CLOSER THAN YOU THINK

by

Peter Murcott

Freely Adapted From An

Old Russian Christmas Story

MOORLEY'S BIBLE & Bookshop Ltd.

CLOSER THAN YOU THINK

by Peter Murcott

A free adaptation from an Old Russian Christmas Story

CHARACTERS

Joseph - who also plays the parts as Old Man and
Woodcutter

Mary   - who also plays the Woodcutter's Wife

Baboushka	First King
Narrator	Second King
First Friend	Third King
Anna (Second Friend)	First Servant
Third Friend	Second Servant

Third Servant

* * * * * * * * * *

If scenery is required, a backcloth showing mountains
and pinewood forests, covered in snow, with a castle
in the distance and small wooden huts or cottages
nearby would suffice throughout the play. There should
be numerous stars in the sky, but the star that the
Kings are following is an imaginary one, off-stage.

The essential props are: a Christmas tree, partly
decorated, with other decorations available; a rather
battered star for the tree; one or two wooden chairs;
a 'treasure chest' with a bag of gold and a bag of sil-
ver coins in it, together with other 'valuables'; a
cradle for the prince; numerous parcels, wrapped in
fancy paper; a bundle of firewood and loose sticks; a
walking stick and a doll to represent the Baby Jesus.

A choir of children is needed for the songs and carols.

* * * * * * * * * *

CLOSER THAN YOU THINK

by Peter Murcott

A free adaptation from an Old Russian Christmas Story

SCENE ONE

(The scene is set in a Russian peasant woman's home
on Christmas Eve. She is expecting guests for a party
and, at the beginning of the play, is decorating her
Christmas Tree)

NARRATOR: Our story begins on Christmas Eve. The
            snow was falling gently on the Russian
            pinewood forests. In a cottage in a tiny
            village, Baboushka was making the final
            preparations for a party.

SONG:

Boys	Girls
Was this just another Christmas? -	No, this was a special Christmas -
Parties, merriment and cheer?	More than merriment and cheer;
Or would she hear,	For she would hear,
Amidst her joy and mirth,	Amidst her joy and mirth,
The message of the birth	The message of the birth
Of Jesus Christ on earth?	Or Jesus Christ on earth,
Or would she hear,	For she would hear,
Amidst her joy and mirth,	Amidst her joy and mirth,
The message of the birth	The message of the birth
Of Christ on earth?	Of Christ on earth.

            (Music at back of Book)

BABOUSHKA: (Standing back from the Christmas tree)
            Thank goodness that's finished. I don't
            think it looks too bad, even though I
            say so myself. (She glances at the clock)
            Just look at the time! My friends will
            be here at any moment and I'm not ready
            yet. I'll just go and .... (a knock is
            heard) Oh, no, there's the first guest.

            (She moves across the stage to open the
            door. Enter Three Kings. They bow)

BABOUSHKA: Oh, who are you? I thought you were my
            friends.... Where are you from?

- 4 -

1ST KING: We are travellers from the East.

2ND KING: We are following a star.

BABOUSHKA: A star! (She glances outside and looks
              up at the sky) But which one? There are
              millions of stars up there. Anyway this
              is no night for travellers.

2ND KING: Ah, but this is no ordinary star. Come!
              (They move outside the house) Look, there
              is the star we are following. (He points
              off-stage) It will lead us to a new-born
              King in Bethlehem. Will you come with us?

BABOUSHKA: To Bethlehem? It sounds an awfully long
              way and, besides, I am expecting some fri-
              ends for a party. I'll tell you what:
              come inside and join us for the evening
              and we'll travel together tomorrow.

1ST KING: Tomorrow! No, it will be too late then.
              Listen, I can hear singing. We are closer
              than you think to the Baby.

CAROL:
        1.   Not far to travel now, wise men,
                  For Bethlehem's in sight;
                  The star alone points to the home
                  Of God's Eternal Light.

        2.   Not long to wait now, Simeon,
                  To bless the Holy Child
                  Whom prophets told — your arms will hold
                  The Saviour, undefiled.

        3.   No need for us to hesitate
                  Or crave a heavenly sign:
                  Christ seeks again His Bethlehem
                  In your heart and in mine.

1ST KING:	Do come with us, Baboushka. <u>(She shakes her head)</u> Very well, we must be on our way. But first we will leave you with these truths from God's Word. Remember them; they will help you to find the new-born King:
	"Those that seek me early shall find me."
2ND KING:	"He that hath pity on the poor lendeth to the Lord."
3RD KING:	"There is a friend that sticketh closer than a brother."
KINGS: <u>(Together)</u>	He's closer than you think, Baboushka. Farewell.
	<u>(They bow and depart. Meanwhile, the first friend arrives)</u>
1ST FRIEND:	Hello, Baboushka, who were those strange men?
BABOUSHKA:	Oh, did you see them? They looked like Kings; yet they said they were looking for a new-born King. It sounds as if he is somewhere close by.
1ST FRIEND:	A new-born King? I haven't heard of one round here, and I'm usually the first to hear of news like that.
	<u>(Second friend, Anna, arrives)</u>
1ST FRIEND:	Look, here's Anna. I say, have you heard anything about a new-born King?
ANNA:	No, not about a <u>King</u>; but I have heard there's a new baby prince in the castle just across the valley. Perhaps he's the one.
BABOUSHKA:	He could be. After all, they did say that he's closer than you think.
ANNA:	Well, he's the one, then.

<u>(Third Friend arrives)</u>

3RD FRIEND: Hello, what are you all talking about?

ANNA: Baboushka's heard there is a new-born King in these parts. We've decided that he must be the new prince over the valley. Have you heard of any other royal baby?

3RD FRIEND: No; none. Still, I must say that I did notice a rather bright star on my way here. Some say that stars only shine like that on important occasions; but I wouldn't know about that. My, it's jolly cold out here.

BABOUSHKA: <u>(shivering)</u> Yes, I'm cold, too. Come in-side, there's a roaring fire in the Kit-chen and lots to eat.

<u>(They follow her across the stage and disappear)</u>

CAROL:

1. Sing for joy, the Saviour's born!
Come see Him now, come see Him now;
Sing for joy, the Saviour's born!
Come see Him in the stable.

   CHORUS
   Peace on earth, goodwill to men
   Our Saviour brings, our Saviour brings;
   Peace on earth, goodwill to men —
   Come see Him in the stable.

2. Hasten, shepherds, and wise men, too,
Come see Him now, come see Him now;
Hasten, shepherds, and wise men, too,
Come see Him in the stable.

3. Spread the message around the world:
"Come see Him now, come see Him now."
Spread the message around the world:
"Come see Him in the stable."

NARRATOR: Strangely enough, Baboushka thought no more about the royal visitors or the new-born King that year. In fact, it was only the following Christmas, when she was once again decorating the tree, that she remembered them.

(Baboushka enters with a rather battered star for the Christmas tree)

BABOUSHKA: (holding the star up against the tree) This star looks rather battered. Star? (She ponders) Wait a minute! I wonder what happened to those Kings last year? (She looks outside at the sky) There are millions of stars shining again, but there's no sign of that special one. I know, I'll have a go at searching for the baby on my own.

(She moves across the stage to her 'treasure chest' near the tree)

NARRATOR: So she went to her treasure chest where she found some gold coins. (She lifts them out) They were very precious to her, so she felt sure they would be good enough as a present. Next she put on a warm cloak and set off.

(She does this and then moves across the stage as if on a journey and then gazes up at the sky)

SONG: (Searching)

Baboushka and Girls	Boys
I'm searching for my King,	O, maiden, take your treasure store
To Him my wealth I'll bring;	And seek your King amidst the poor;
I know He's calling me,	That's where He bids you be,
But where, O where is He?	For such a birth had He.
He's calling, calling,	Go seek Him, seek Him,
I know He's calling me.	His face at last you'll see.
He's calling, calling,	Go seek Him, seek Him,
I know He's calling me.	His face at last you'll see.

END OF SCENE ONE

- 8 -

(The scene is set in the castle over the
valley. It is the prince's first birthday,
and the servants are making preparations
for his party. The prince is lying in a
cradle, surrounded by presents)

1ST SERVANT: (bustling around) Oh, it's this for the
prince and that for the prince. Do you
know, I've been rushed off my poor feet -
and all for the prince!

2ND SERVANT: Just look at all his presents - nnd he's
only one year old. It seems silly to me,
making all this fuss. How can he possibly
know what it's all about?

(1st Servant pauses, walks across to the
cradle and wags his finger at the baby)

1ST SERVANT: I hope you realise what you've done to my
poor feet, all through running round after
your birthday party.

(The Prince starts to cry)

2ND SERVANT: Now look what you've done! You'll be for
it if you don't quieten him down.

1ST SERVANT: (soothingly) There, there. Prince, prince,
prince, prince, stop crying, prince!

(The Prince carries on crying)

2ND SERVANT: It's no use making that row; you'll only
make him worse.

(A knock is heard at the door. The 2nd
Servant opens it and returns with
Baboushka)

1ST SERVANT: Who's this woman? You know you're not
supposed to bring strangers in here.

BABOUSHKA: (timidly) I've come to see the prince,
if I may?

(1st Servant looks her up and down)

1ST SERVANT: Are you a princess? You don't look like a princess, or anyone important, for that matter. We're not allowed to let the prince see strangers - unless, that is, they are important.

BABOUSHKA: My name's Baboushka. No, I'm not a princess, but I am looking for a new-born King; and I've brought him a present.

2ND SERVANT: (pondering) Baboushka? Baboushka? 'Can't say I've heard of you. Mind you, its very kind of you to bring the prince a present. (Looks at the 1st Servant) What shall we do?

(3rd Servant enters)

3RD SERVANT: What's going on? Why aren't you working? Who's this woman? Is she causing trouble?

2ND SERVANT: She's called Baboushka, and she says she's brought the prince a present.

3RD SERVANT: (haughtily) Oh, I'm sorry, the prince never accepts presents from strangers. I mean, well, I don't want to appear rude, but one cannot be too careful nowadays. (Turns to 1st Servant) Anyway, it's Tuesday. (winks)

1ST SERVANT: (puzzled) Tuesday! So what?

3RD SERVANT: You know there's an old royal superstition: never accept presents on Tuesdays.

2ND SERVANT: (brightly) But today's Wednesday!

3RD SERVANT: (glaring) You'll be having a present in a minute, if I hear another word from you! (Turning to Baboushka) Sorry, dear. (He ushers her to the door) Call again sometime.

(She leaves and he heaves a sigh of relief)

3RD SERVANT: Now then, you two, it's time for the Royal Bath. Bring His Royal Highness at once.

(They all leave, carrying the cradle)

- 10 -

1. Dark was the night —
The trav'llers were weary,
No rest in sight —
The prospect looked dreary;
Then Mary sighed:
"It seems that tonight
We'll have to sleep out in the cold."

2. From door to door:
"Oh, please can you spare me? ..."
"Sorry, no more!"
Poor Joseph and Mary
Were close to despair,
When, seeing their plight,
An innkeeper lent them a stall.

3. So humble a birth
For Jesus — a stable;
Still millions on earth
Need those who are able
To find them a home;
Remember, the Light
Of the World bids you come to their aid.

End of Scene Two

Scene Three

NARRATOR: On her way home, Baboushka met an old man.

(They enter from opposite directions)

OLD MAN: You look sad. Where are you going?

BABOUSHKA: Nowhere in particular. I've just been
trying to find a new-born King. I wanted
to give him a present.

OLD MAN: Have you tried the castle?

BABOUSHKA: Yes; but the servants there wouldn't even
let me see the baby prince.

OLD MAN: Ah, you would have done better had you been
able to see the King himself first — but
he's so busy nowadays.

BABOUSHKA: I suppose I'd better take this present home
now. (She looks hard at the Old Man who is
poorly dressed) No, I'd like you to have it.

(She hands him the money)

OLD MAN: (looking at the coins) But these are valuable.

BABOUSHKA: All the more reason why you should have them.
I feel much better now. I hope you have a
happy Christmas.

OLD MAN: Thank you, my dear, and the same to you.
May God bless you.

(They both leave the stage in opposite
directions)

NARRATOR:	The following year she decided to try again. This time she had found some silver coins which were tied carefully in a small bag. She decided whe would search through a near-by forest for some clue about the Baby King. As she was doing this, a poor woodcutter and his wife were making their way home.

(Enter woodcutter and his wife, gathering sticks. The woodcutter is carrying a bundle of firewood)

WOODCUTTER:	There's hardly enough wood here for a fire for ourselves, let alone any for sale.
WIFE:	What shall we tell the children? We've nothing to sell, so we can't make any money. What sort of Christmas can we give them this year?
WOODCUTTER:	(putting down his bundle) I don't know! I had hoped we might be able to manage a few small presents - but now we can't even afford the food.
WIFE:	Well, talking won't make things better. Let's go home; I'm absolutely frozen.
WOODCUTTER:	Let's rest a moment first. I'm exhausted.

(They both sit down. Meanwhile, Baboushka, who has overheard part of the conversation, slips up, unseen, behind them and places the bag of money on the bundle of sticks and then creeps away)

WOODCUTTER:	Right, then, I'm ready. (He turns to pick up the sticks) Hello, what's this?

(He picks up the bag of money)

WIFE:	Look, there's a piece of paper with it, too. (She reads) "I hope you have a happier Christmas - from a friend."
WOODCUTTER:	(opening the bag) Ten silver coins! We've never had so much money. Wait until we tell the children.

(They both leave happily)

Boys

O, maiden, take your treasure store
And seek your King amidst the poor;
That's where He bids you be,
For such a birth had He.
Go seek Him, seek Him,
His face at last you'll see.
Go seek Him, seek Him,
His face at last you'll see.

End of Scene Three

Scene Four

(Back in Baboushka's cottage)

NARRATOR: So the years passed by. Each Christmas Baboushka went to her treasure chest and chose a gift for the new-born King whom she never found. Each year her gifts brought happiness to someone in need.

(A brief mime could take place during the above paragraph of Baboushka handing out gifts to the poor)

At last she had little left of value. She was growing old, and she felt the wind too keenly to venture out at Christmas time.

(She enters, using a walking stick, and sits on a chair near the Christmas tree)

One Christmas Eve, when she was sitting all alone, thinking of all her apparently fruitless journeys, she heard a knock at the door.

(A knock is heard. Baboushka rises slowly and reaches for her stick)

BABOUSHKA: Who can that be at this time of night?

(She opens the door, and the Three Kings enter and bow)

1ST KING: Greetings, Baboushka, we're so glad to see you again, and we are so happy that you followed our advice. Do you remember? -

"Those that seek me early shall find me."

2ND KING: "He that hath pity on the poor lendeth to the Lord."

- 13 -

3RD KING: "There is a friend that sticketh closer than a brother."

1ST KING: And you found the new-born King!

BABOUSHKA: But that is what I've failed to do all these past years.

2ND KING: But you _did_ find him.

(_Mary and Joseph enter with the Baby Jesus in Mary's arms. They are the same characters as the Old Man, the Woodcutter and his wife_)

2ND KING: Look carefully at their faces. Haven't you seen them somewhere before?

JOSEPH: "Inasmuch as ye have done it unto the least of these my brethren, (_he points to the baby_) ye have done it unto me."

MARY: (_beckoning_) Come and see the new-born King, the Saviour of the World. He's been closer to you than a brother for many years, Baboushka. He is close to all who seek to serve Him. Oh, if but more people knew it, He's closer than you think.

CAROL:

Three Kings - each brings
A gift for Jesus: gold most rare,
Incense and myrrh.
O that I could have been there!

What Light that night
Came down to earth to show God's care
For all people.
O that I could have been there!

2. Each King, kneeling
Within the stable cold and bare,
Worshipped Jesus.
O that I could have been there!

4. But I know my
Dear Lord can still be found today:
Seek Him! Love Him!
Walk for ever in His Way!

THE END

WOULD SHE HEAR?

NOT FAR TO TRAVEL

1. Not far to travel now, wise men, For Bethlehem's in sight;
The star alone points to the home Of God's Eternal Light.

© From More Sing for Jesus

COME SEE HIM

1. Sing for joy, the Saviour's born! Come see Him now, come see Him now;
2. Hasten, shepherds, and wise men. too, Come see Him now, come see Him now;
3. Spread the message around the world: Come see Him now, come see Him now;

1. Sing for joy the Saviour's born. Come see Him in the stable.
2. Hasten, shepherds, and wise men, too, Come see Him in the stable.
3. Spread the message around the world: Come see Him in the stable.

Peace on earth, goodwill to men Our Saviour brings, our Saviour brings;

Peace on earth, goodwill to men - Come see Him in the stable.

SEARCHING

Introduction to V.1 only

I'm searching for my King..... To Him my wealth I'll bring.... I know He's calling me..... But where, O where is

He?...... He's calling, calling, I

know He's calling me. He's calling,

calling, I know He's calling me.

GOD'S HOMELESS

CAPO ON
FRET 3

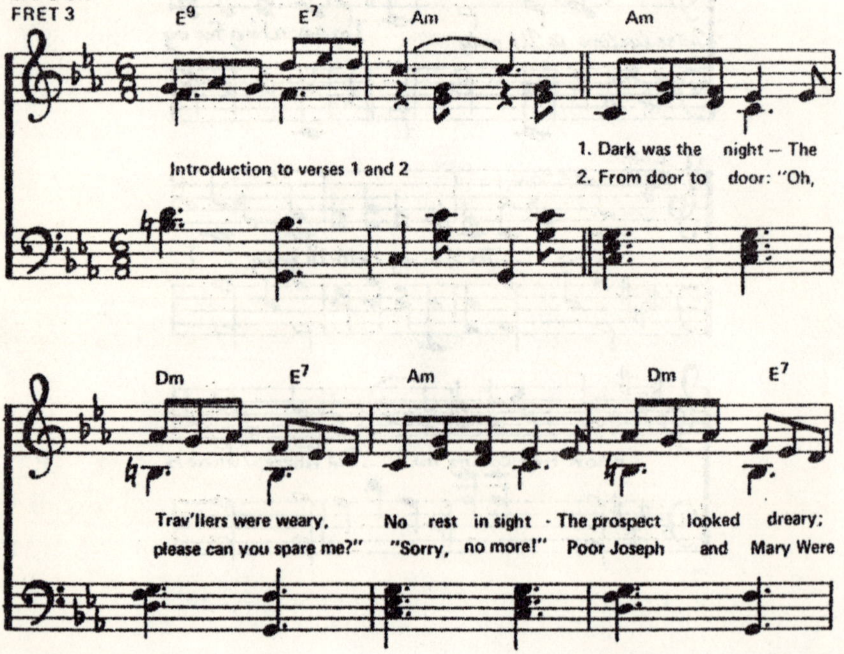

E⁹ E⁷ Am Am

Introduction to verses 1 and 2

1. Dark was the   night – The
2. From door to   door: "Oh,

Dm E⁷ Am Dm E⁷

Trav'llers were weary,   No   rest in sight - The prospect   looked   dreary;
please can you spare me?"   "Sorry, no more!"   Poor Joseph   and   Mary Were

Then Mary sighed: "It seems that tonight   We'll have to sleep out in the cold."

close to despair,   When, seeing their plight,   An   innkeeper lent them a   stall.

Introduction to verse 3   (3) So   humble   a   birth For

Jesus -   a   stable;   Still millions   on   earth   Need those who are   able   To

find them a home;   Remember, the Light Of the world   bids you come to their aid

THREE KINGS

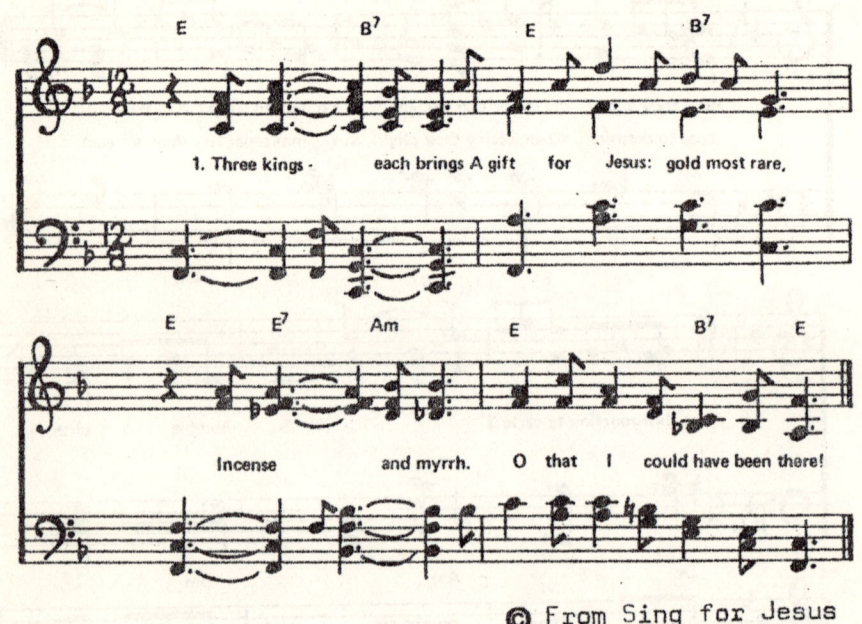

1. Three kings - each brings A gift for Jesus: gold most rare,
Incense and myrrh. O that I could have been there!

Making Greenhouses

R. H. WARRING

Model & Allied Publications Ltd
13–35 Bridge Street, Hemel Hempstead, Herts
England

Model & Allied Publications Limited,
Book Division,
Station Road, Kings Langley,
Hertfordshire, England.

First Published 1973

ISBN 0 85242 326 8

Printed and made in England by
Page Bros (Norwich) Ltd, Norwich, Norfolk.

Contents

Types of Greenhouses 1

The traditional type of greenhouse is of rectangular 'box' shape with a span roof. It is, in fact, correctly referred to as a span roof type. Although the basic shape is the same, there are three main variations, as shown in Fig. 1.1, differing only in the amount of glass in the walls and ends.

With the glass-to-the-ground type there is maximum light penetration through the sides. This is particularly suitable for growing tall plants directly from the soil, or from pots stood on the ground—such as tomatoes, chrysanthemums and greenhouse climbers. It can also be fitted with permanent or temporary staging for carrying small plants. The only real disadvantage is that the large glass area means that more heating is required in winter to maintain the interior temperature, if a warm greenhouse is required (see also Chapter 8).

Fig. 1.1   SPAN GREENHOUSES

GLASS TO GROUND   BRICK WALLS   HALF-BOARDED
(5 OR 6 BRICKS HIGH)
DWARF WALL

In the other two variations the depth of glass is reduced by introducing side walls, or boarding in the lower half of the sides and ends. This will conserve heat and also provide a shaded area for over-wintering tubers and corms, resting plants, or forcing others as required. Alternatively the lower sections may be used for storing pots, etc. The main 'growing area' is provided by staging erected at wall level or slightly above (see also Chapter 6).

The span roof greenhouse, therefore, is a general-purpose type which can readily be adapted to various growing needs. If the extra cost of heating is not significant, the glass-to-ground variant is usually the best, as well as the most economical to erect in the first place. It is certainly the most versatile as regards the growing conditions which can be provided, and shading can always be provided when necessary (again, see Chapter 7).

The Dutch greenhouse is another 'all-glass' house, but with inward sloping sides and even larger glass area—Fig. 1.2. Again it is particularly suited for growing plants directly from the ground, or in pots at ground level, but can of course be fitted with staging. Heat loss in winter is rather greater than a span roof type of the same size; and the amount of glass and base area required is also greater for the same volume.

The shape, however, is more modern and attractive and often appeals as an alternative to the glass-to-ground span roof type because of this. A disadvantage is that very large sheets of glass are involved, which can make erection more difficult—and breakages more expensive.

Fig. 1.2

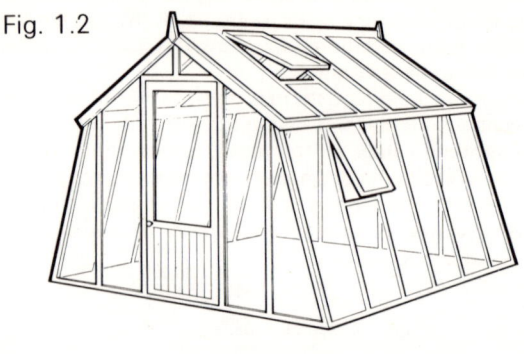

DUTCH GREENHOUSE

Fig. 1.3

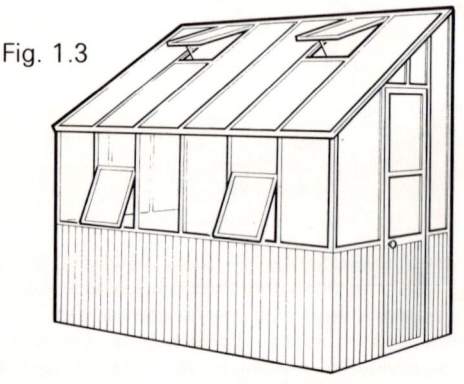

LEAN-TO GREENHOUSE

The other basic type is the *lean-to* greenhouse, designed to be erected against an existing wall. This reduces the amount of material required, and at the same time the existing wall can provide shelter and stability. Heating costs are reduced, but the value of such a greenhouse is greatly influenced by siting (see later).

The usual type of lean-to is of semi-span construction, with glass-to-ground, or dwarf wall or half boarded—Fig. 1.3. Space may be somewhat restricted as a consequence, particularly if the house is made on the narrow side. Every effort should be made to ensure that there is enough width for plants to be trained up the wall, as well as utilising staging on the glass wall—and still leave comfortable room for working.

If the width can be extended considerably, and the existing wall is suitable, a three-quarter span house may provide a better solution—Fig. 1.4. This extends the shape to almost 'full' greenhouse width, but the extra area will not be worthwhile unless properly lighted. Construction is also more complicated, but the cost is still less than that of a normal span house.

Fig. 1.4

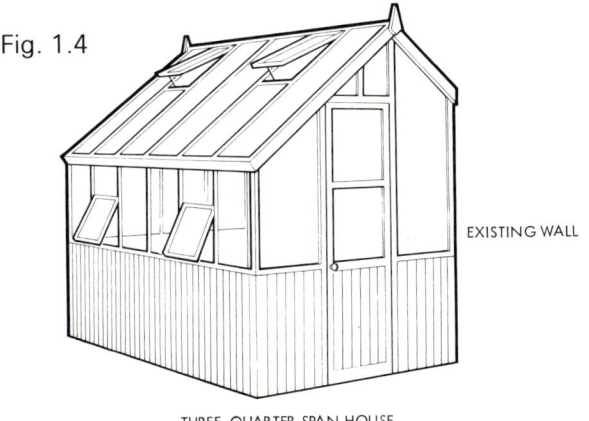

EXISTING WALL

THREE-QUARTER SPAN HOUSE

Fig. 1.5   Fig. 1.6

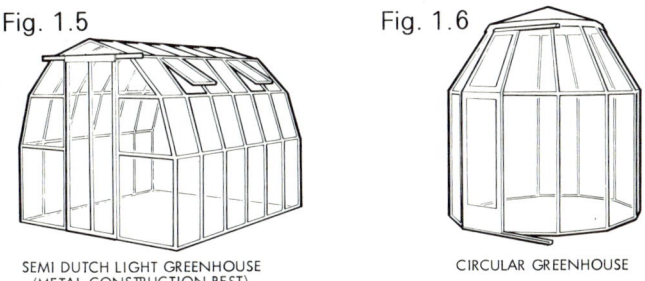

SEMI DUTCH LIGHT GREENHOUSE
(METAL CONSTRUCTION BEST)   CIRCULAR GREENHOUSE

There are, of course, many other possible greenhouse shapes. A variation on the 'Dutch light' principle is shown in Fig. 1.5, providing an extensive glass area designed to catch maximum light in winter, provided it is properly sited. Structurally it also incorporates additional beams which may be advantageous—or even necessary—on a metal greenhouse, as well as splitting up the glazed area into economic panel sizes.

A much more unusual shape is shown in Fig. 1.6—a circular greenhouse. The main appeal of this is probably its novelty, although it does also provide good all-round light. However, the working area in this case is greatly reduced. Construction is also more complicated, particularly as regards the glass shapes required for the roof, but such shapes are available in prefabricated 'kit' form for amateur erection.

In addition conventional greenhouse forms are often allied to other garden buildings. This is usually applied to span roof types where one part of the house, for example, is boarded off and separated with an interior partition to provide an integral tool shed or potting shed. Some types of conservatories and house extensions, too, are basically of greenhouse form, or can be used as greenhouses, particularly if clear glass is used for the roofing instead of obscure wired glass or semi-opaque plastic which can reduce light and 'draw' seedlings.

Siting

Siting a greenhouse is important. Wherever possible it should be located clear of all shade, in a position where it receives maximum light from the sun and sky. It is easy to reduce excessively strong sunlight by shading a greenhouse, but virtually impossible to make up for lack of lighting except at considerable expense (e.g. with selected artificial lighting).

The generally recommended *orientation* for a free standing greenhouse is normally East to West—Fig. 1.7. This allows the house to receive maximum benefit from low winter sun—provided, of course, it is not shaded in this direction by other buildings. In this case the south-facing side of the greenhouse will receive the most light, and is the side on which glass-to-ground glazing is preferred. The north side wall can be half boarded to reduce heat losses.

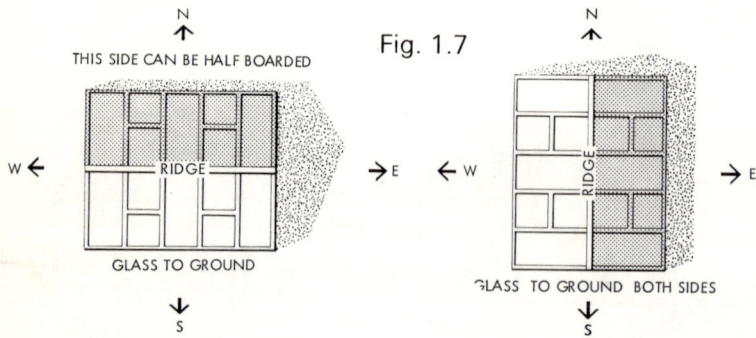

Fig. 1.7

Alternatively siting with the ridge running in a North-South direction is good, especially for a glass-to-ground house. Both sides will then receive an equal amount of sunlight. Shading is often difficult to avoid in small gardens, but as far as possible no compromise should be accepted. The greenhouse should be sited where it will receive the maximum possible amount of sky light at all seasons.

Several other pratical points need to be considered. These can be dealt with briefly.
(i) A *sheltered* position is desirable since this can considerably reduce the amount of heating required in winter. Also it can reduce the risk of structural damage occurring in gales, etc. But shelter should not be accepted if this also means *shading*.
(ii) Location away from boundary walls, or proximity to neighbouring trees should be avoided, even if the latter does not give direct shading. This can reduce the likelihood of damage to the glass through objects thrown over a wall, or falling branches, etc.

(iii) Convenience should also be considered. On cold winter days it is far more convenient to have the greenhouse close at hand to the house than away at the bottom of the garden! Also siting near the house will simplify, and lower the cost of, laying on water and electricity supplies to the greenhouse. Again, however, an unshaded position should take precedence over convenience.

(iv) Site the greenhouse in a relatively dry position—not on ground which can become waterlogged or flooded during winter. An excessively damp atmosphere in the greenhouse can be ruinous in winter—and waterlogged soil can cause foundations to sag.

(v) Locate the greenhouse on a level site. This will simplify foundation work.

(vi) Plan a suitable approach to the greenhouse. In winter ground will be wet and soggy. A path or stepping stones will provide dry access to the greenhouse in inclement weather.

Siting a Lean-to Greenhouse

The best site for a lean-to greenhouse is on a South wall, a West wall, or an East wall, in that order—Fig. 1.8. A North wall is very poor since the house will generally receive little or no winter sun; and very little summer sun unless the wall is no higher than the greenhouse (e.g. a garage wall). An East wall is not much better as although it should receive good morning light in the winter, the strength of the sunlight will be lower than that received by a South or West facing lean-to on a similar site.

Fig. 1.8

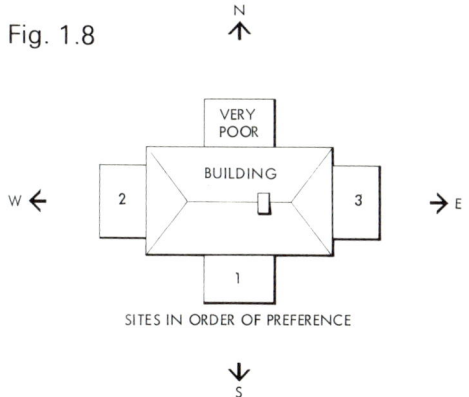

SITES IN ORDER OF PREFERENCE

Unfortunately walls against which a lean-to can be built very seldom face south or west, so it may have to be a matter of compromise, or even accepting whatever site *is* available. The rule then is to favour a South to West facing wall whenever possible. Any other facing is likely to seriously limit the performance achieved by plants and seedlings in the greenhouse, unless choice is restricted to certain types. For example, a lean-to (or any other greenhouse for that matter) which *has* to be sited in partial shade can still produce good results with shade-loving plants.

Shading is often a particular problem with a lean-to greenhouse, since its position is fixed by existing walls of adjacent buildings, and this can be modified by the height of the wall. A lean-to on the South face of a fairly tall house, for example, will probably be largely shaded by the house from summer sun—Fig. 1.9. Try to work out the shade pattern likely to be cast by the house, or adjacent buildings, during the seasons and try to locate the lean-to on the wall which received the maximum amount of sky light.

Lack of light will mean that the early season's growings will be delayed—offsetting much of the advantages offered by a heated greenhouse in winter. Initial growth, too, will tend to be weak, with spindly seedlings developing which have little or no hope of growing into robust plants. Light *during the seed growing time* is of particular importance. Bear this in mind in siting the lean-to greenhouse if you want to start seeds in January, February and March whilst the sun is still relatively low in the southern sky.

Fig. 1.9

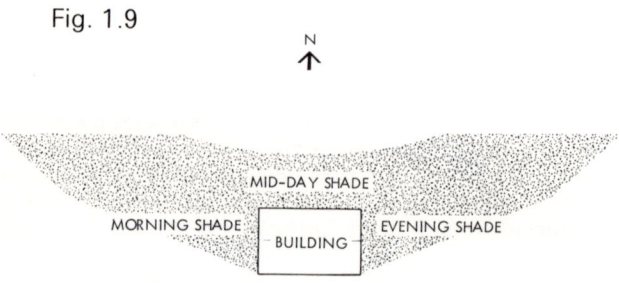

Materials

Greenhouse frames can be made of timber or metal. Timber is more suitable for amateur construction and is generally cheaper. Metal greenhouses offer the advantage of complete durability with minimum maintenance and can be built up from standard metal sections without being an expert in metalworking. A simpler solution in the latter case, however, is usually to buy a prefabricated greenhouse where all the metal sections are cut to length, predrilled, and largely pre-assembled in panels.

Prefabricated greenhouses are also available in wood. The deciding factor may be overall cost. Size for size, a wood greenhouse will be cheaper than a metal greenhouse; and a greenhouse built from scratch will be cheaper than a prefabricated kit (the difference usually being greater with a wooden house than a metal house). If cost is not the main factor, then the great advantage of a prefabricated greenhouse (in wood or metal) is the considerable saving in time taken to complete the building.

In the case of a timber greenhouse, the woods used are red cedar, redwood and softwoods. Red cedar is generally regarded as the best timber, but is also the most expensive. It can also vary a lot in quality. For first class work—and maximum durability—the additional cost of first class red cedar is well worthwhile. It is a timber which is not susceptible to rot and, in fact, needs no finishing treatment. However in this case the attractive red colour of the wood will rapidly age to a dull grey colour due to weathering. It is thus preferable to treat the finished framework with a cedar preservative which will both help maintain the colour and also act as a water repellant. This is a much simpler method than painting, and even more effective in waterproofing the wood. There is, of course, no reason why cedar should not be painted in white or colour to match other buildings.

Redwood is another fully acceptable building timber, offering a saving of about 10 per cent over cedar. The actual timber sold as 'redwood' is usually *red deal*—a northern European and Russian softwood. It is yellow rather than red in colour, and is usually best painted fo finish. However, it can be made to look like cedar by painting with a redwood sealer. Select one which is stated to be a water repellant preservative.

The use of ordinary softwood can offer a saving of about 25 per cent over cedar. However, commercial softwood is often far from properly seasoned and, even if painted, may rot in as little as four or five years. It is also susceptible to warping. The initial economy offered by softwoods, therefore, is seldom worthwhile. There may be the exception, and, in fact, some prefabricated greenhouses are produced in softwoods at about 75 per cent of the cost of a similar kit in redwood or cedar. The best advice that can be offered with softwood construction is that it must be properly painted and the paintwork maintained in good condition—when it could give a long and satisfactory life.

Metal Greenhouses

High tensile aluminium is the preferred material for greenhouse frames, produced in the form of extruded strip. Aluminium is non-corroding and requires no maintenance. If necessary it can be painted to match an existing building, but in this case will require a preliminary coating of etching primer if the paint coating is to be durable. Painting straight on plain aluminium will result in the paint peeling off in a relatively short time.

A particular advantage offered by aluminium sections is that the material is strong and rigid and so the various frame members can be quite slender, increasing the amount of open or glazed area. Aluminium frames are also light, which can make lifting in place and assembly easier.

Steel or iron sections can also be used, again having the advantage of high strength in the sections. However the types of sections available are more limited; also drilling and cutting is more difficult. Ferrous metal sections also need protection against rusting by galvanising and/or painting and repainting is generally necessary at fairly frequent intervals. It may be preferred to aluminium for larger metal greenhouses, but aluminium is generally better for the smaller houses usually associated with amateur construction.

Apart from extreme durability, two other important advantages offered by metal greenhouses are that they do not absorb water and the material will not harbour pests. Timber houses, however, tend to remain warmer, especially in winter.

Size

There is no answer as to the 'best' size of greenhouse for the amateur. Basically, the bigger the better for this provides the greatest scope and flexibility of operation. However the larger the size the greater the initial cost—and the greater the cost of heating in winter. But doubling the length of a greenhouse, for example, would increase cost *less* than in simple proportion to the linear dimension, although heating cost would rise in proportion to the increased *volume*.

In terms of cost per square foot of greenhouse, the larger the size the more economic it is. This applies particularly in the case of prefabricated greenhouses; less so with scratch-built houses using basic materials, but here there is a similar benefit in building time (you get more for the hours spent in construction).

The best advice is to decide on an 'oversize' rather than an 'undersize' green-house—i.e. chose a 'maximum' size practical for the site available, material costs involved, and the amount of time available for construction. If it proves too costly to heat during the winter months, part can be partitioned off and made a 'cold' house; or

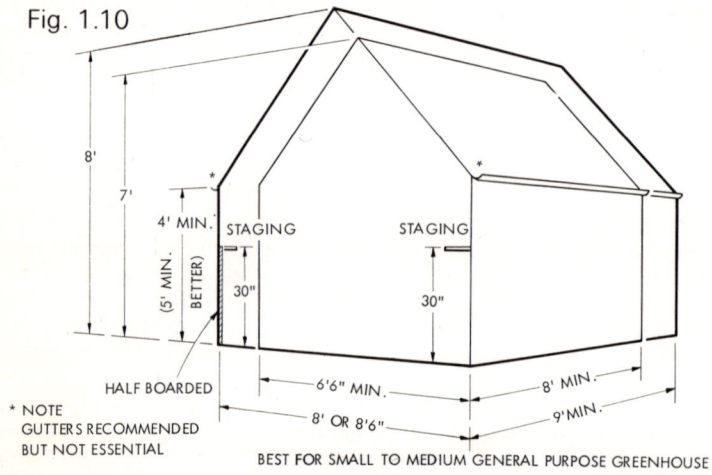

Fig. 1.10

BEST FOR SMALL TO MEDIUM GENERAL PURPOSE GREENHOUSE

the whole can be operated as a 'cold' house. A small greenhouse may seem an attractive proposition, but it can be most frustrating in a year or so. It can rapidly become overcrowded, and performance can suffer as a consequence. The man who starts with a small greenhouse and becomes enthusiastic about greenhouse work nearly always has to build another, larger greenhouse in a few years—or at least double the size of his original house by extension!

Proportions are not all that important, although from the point of view of economic structure and sufficient room for working a minimum height to eaves of 4 ft is required (with 5 ft a preferred minimum for any size of house). A little extra—and very useful—height can often be obtained from the foundations—see Chapter 2.

A good width is important, too, as this gives a lot more planting space. Here the amateur builder starting from scratch is often at an advantage. Proprietary green-house 'kits' are usually based on a limited number of standard widths available in a wider range of different lengths (as a matter of economic production of standard sections utilising similar ends). Most span and Dutch greenhouses of this type are, therefore, usually limited to staging along each side. Extra width can provide space for additional staging in the middle and a lot more 'working area' which is readily accessible without greatly increasing the overall floor area. This may be preferred to a longer greenhouse of 'standard' width—see also Chapter 6.

TYPES OF GREENHOUSES

Specific recommendations for suitable sizes and proportions for amateur construction are summarised in Figs. 1.10, 1.11 and 1.12. A minimum width of 6 ft 6 in. is suggested, with 8 ft or 8 ft 6 in. as an 'optimum' width for a medium size span greenhouse (Fig. 1.10). These would give a height to ridge of 7 ft and 8 ft respectively, in round figures, associated with a height to eaves of 4 ft. The latter again is an

Fig. 1.11

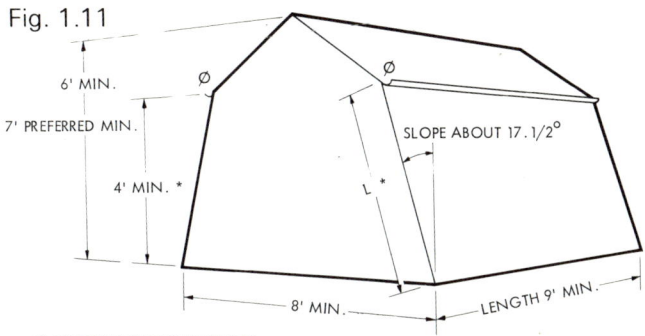

6' MIN.

7' PREFERRED MIN.

SLOPE ABOUT 17.1/2°

4' MIN. *

L *

8' MIN.

LENGTH 9' MIN.

Ø GUTTERING RECOMMENDED

* NOTE.
A STANDARD DUTCH LIGHT
OR L DIMENSION IS 4'8".

Fig. 1.12

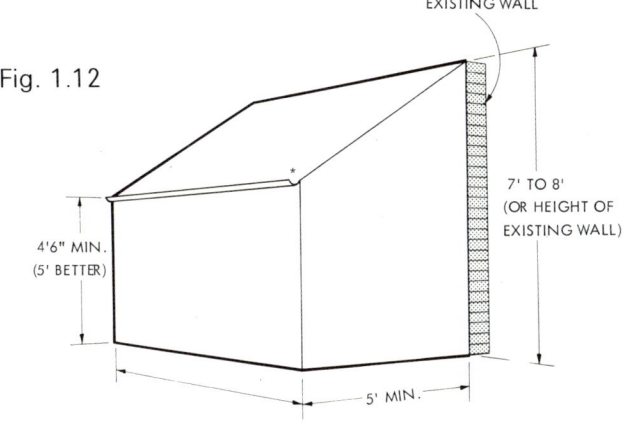

EXISTING WALL

4'6" MIN.
(5' BETTER)

7' TO 8'
(OR HEIGHT OF
EXISTING WALL)

5' MIN.

* GUTTER RECOMMENDED

absolute minimum figure. It would probably be better increased to 5 ft to provide more 'headroom' over the top of interior staging. A 5 ft height to eaves would increase the height to ridge by 1 ft, keeping the pitch of the roof the same. On a larger house, a 6 ft height to eaves would be preferable.

Corresponding minimum lengths are also shown in the diagram—e.g. 8 ft for a 6 ft 6 in. width and 9 ft for an 8 ft or 8 ft 6 in. width. These are nominal dimensions. Length can be increased whilst maintaining the same width and cross section; but for any length exceeding about 13 ft a better proportion would be achieved by adopting an 8 ft minimum width. In other words, once the length exceeds twice the width, the possible advantages in increasing the width proportionally should be investigated— see Chapter 6. From the structural design point of view—and usually both cost of materials and ease of assembly—maintaining minimum widths, as specified, can be advantageous, even if the length required does work out considerably in excess of twice the width.

With a half boarded house the height of the boarding should run to 30 in.; or the height of the staging, if this is greater than 30 in. (see Chapter 6 again). Dwarf walls are often only built to about half this height—say five or six bricks.

Recommended proportions for a Dutch greenhouse are basically similar, except that the roof pitch is less and the sloping sides require more ground level width—see Fig. 1.12. A lean-to greenhouse is rather like a span house cut down the middle. However the minimum width really required is about 5 ft and rather more than 4 ft minimum is required for the height to eaves. A height to ridge of 7 to 8 ft is then a logical figure for a lean-to built against a high wall. Often, however, a lean-to is erected against a lower wall, e.g. against the side of a garage or other single storey building. In this case the height to ridge may be governed by the height of the permanent wall. It cannot project above it. This can also modify the pitch of the roof. If this is drastically reduced, then the height to eaves will have to be reduced to compensate. A roof pitch of less than 30° is not desirable as this can accumulate a potential damaging weight of snow in a heavy winter.

As a further guide, proportions of a number of typical proprietary greenhouses are summarised in Table I.

TABLE I. EXAMPLES OF PROPRIETARY GREENHOUSE SIZES

Maker	Type	Width	Height to Eaves	Height to Ridge	Lengths	Construction
Pratten	Span	10'0"	5'5"	8'0"	12'10"–19'0"	Wood on Brick walls
	Dutch	7'0" & 8'6"	4'10"	7'2"	8'6"–10'7"	Wood
Humex	Circular	8'0" dia.	6'0"	7'6"	—	Metal
Hebditch	Span	5'0", 7'0" & 8'0"	4'6"	7'0"	7'0"–15'8"	Cedar
Critall	Span	10'0"	5'1"	7'6"	12'3"–54'10"	Galv. Steel
	Span	8'6"	5'1"	7'1"	6'2"–28'6"	Galv. Steel
	Dutch	6'3"	5'0"	7'0"	6'3" & 8'3"	Aluminium
	Lean-to	5'0"–9'3"	5'1"	7'6"–9'5"	6'2"–30'6"	Galv. Steel
Regal	Span	12'0"	5'0"	8'6"	12'10"–50'9"	Cedar
	Span	8'0"	5'0"	7'6"	Any	Cedar
	Dutch	6'0"	—	—	5'1"–15'2"	Cedar
Park Lines	Span	6'4" & 8'7"	4'2"	7'2"	10'5"–14'7"	Cedar or Softwoods
	Lean-to	4'3" & 6'4"	6'6"	8'0"	6'4"–12'6"	Cedar or Softwoods
Eden	Span	8'4¼"	4'6"	7'6"	8'4½"–12'5"	Aluminium
	Lean-to	6'3"	5'0"	7'6"	8'4" & 12'5"	Aluminium
Banbury	Span	5'9"	4'10"	6'1"	5'1"–19'9½"	Wood on Concrete Walls
		7'6½"	4'10"	7'6"	5'1"–19'9½"	Wood on Concrete Walls
		12'0"	4'10"	8'4"	5'1"–19'9½"	Wood on Concrete Walls
	Span	5'9"	4'10"	6'11"	5'1"–19'9½"	Cedar
		7'6½"	4'10"	7'6"	5'1"–19'9½"	Cedar
		12'0"	4'10"	8'9"	5'1"–19'9½".	Cedar
	Span	6'2¼"	5'4½"	7'2¼"	5'3½"–20'3½"	Cedar
		7'7¾"	5'4½"	7'7¾"	5'3½"–20'3½"	Cedar
		9'8¾"	5'4½"	9'8¾"	5'3½"–20'3½"	Cedar
	Span	6'2¼"	5'4½"	7'2¼"	5'3½"–20'3½"	Aluminium
		7'7¾"	5'4½"	7'7¾"	5'3½"–20'3½"	Aluminium
		9'8¾"	5'4½"	8'2"	5'3½"–20'3½"	Aluminium
Oakwood (Worth)	Span	5'2"	4'8"	6'4"	6'2"–9'9"	Oak & Cedar
	Span	6'0"	4'8"	6'6"	6'2"–11'9"	Oak & Cedar
	Span	8'3"	4'8"	7'3"	8'2"–18'11"	Oak & Cedar
Alton	Dutch	8'5"	5'6"	7'2"	8'0"–15'7"	Cedar or Deal
	Dutch	10'0"	5'6"	7'6"	10'6"–20'7"	Cedar or Deal
Compton	Span	5'8½"	4'10¾"	6'8"	7'6"–19'10"	Cedar
	Lean-to	6'4"	6'0"	7'9¼"	5'3½"–15'3½"	Cedar
Halls	Span	5'0"	4'0"	5'6"	6'0"	Cedar, Half Boarded
	Span	6'4½"	4'0"	6'10"	6'5"–11'0"	Cedar
	Span	8'4½"	4'0"	7'8"	8'7"–29'5"	Cedar
	Dutch	8'0"	4'0"	6'0"	8'7"–21'1"	Cedar
	Dutch	10'0"	5'0"	7'0"	12'5"–30'1"	Cedar
Waltons	Span	5'0" to 12'0"	5'0"	7'0"–9'0"	8'0" to 30'0"	Timber, half Boarded
	Lean-to	5'0" to 10'0"	5'0"	7'9"–9'0"	8'0" to 20'0"	Timber, Half Boarded
	Dutch	8'4"	5'7"	7'6"	8'6"–12'8"	Timber
Cedarworth (Worth)	Dutch	6'9"	5'3"	6'5"	5'6"–13'0"	Cedar
	Dutch	8'1"	5'3"	6'9"	8'0"–15'6"	Cedar
	Dutch	16'3"	5'3"	7'2"	13'0"–18'0"	Cedar

Foundations 2

Any greenhouse needs a good solid foundation on a level site, but the foundations are only required to support the walls. It is also desirable that the wall frames be permanently fixed to the foundations. Although the glazed house will be quite heavy, it could be displaced by a strong wind if not secured to its foundations and the resulting damage could be very expensive.

A simple foundation sometimes used with a small greenhouse is solid timber beams rested on bricks and hardcore, as shown in Fig. 2.1. The wood members are treated with preservative, and should preferably be of hardwood. Apart from being very easy to set up such a foundation, fixing of the frames to the wood beams is also very straightforward. This method does, however, have many disadvantages. if the wood rots, then the house is left without a good solid foundation. Also the beam may well develop a sag in the middle of its length in time under the weight of the greenhouse wall (to which the staging is attached), due to subsidence of the hardcore base. More permanent types of foundations are therefore to be preferred.

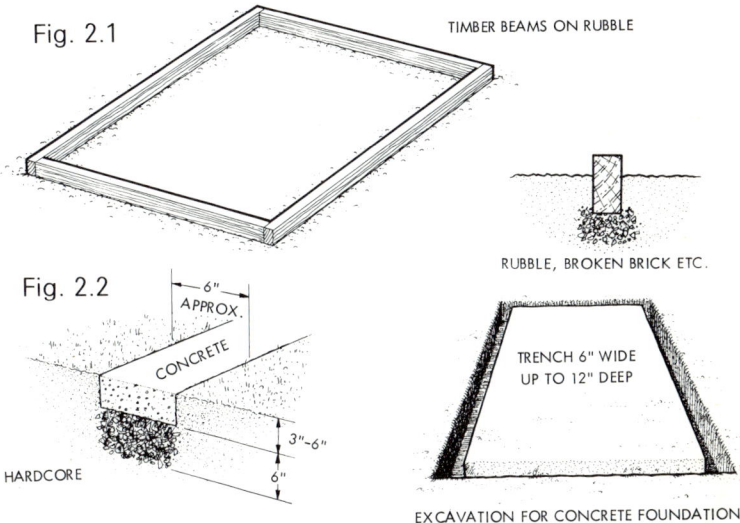

Fig. 2.1

TIMBER BEAMS ON RUBBLE

RUBBLE, BROKEN BRICK ETC.

Fig. 2.2

6"
APPROX.

CONCRETE

3"-6"

HARDCORE

6"

TRENCH 6" WIDE
UP TO 12" DEEP

EXCAVATION FOR CONCRETE FOUNDATION

A concrete foundation laid in a trench, the bottom of which is filled with rubble and hardcore is best—Fig. 2.2. The width of the foundation should be about 6 in. (or slightly less for a small greenhouse); and the depth up to 6 in., depending on the size and weight of the greenhouse. The hardcore 'base' should be at least 6 in. deep. The concrete can be poured directly into a neatly excavated trench. If the sides are 'ragged', then a neater foundation will result from using hardboard strips inserted against the sides of the trench flush with the top to act as shuttering. These can be left in situ when the cement has set.

Further treatment then depends on the type of greenhouse being built, and particularly the materials of construction. A metal greenhouse can have its main frames bolted directly to the concrete foundation, in which case suitable bolts with plates can be set in the concrete whilst still wet. It is rather better to erect an additional narrow 'wall' on which the frames rest, since this raises the bottom edge of the glass above soil level (in the case of a glass-to-ground house), where it is less likely to be damaged. Such a wall can be poured onto the original foundation, as shown in Fig. 2.3, using wooden shuttering. Again the fastening bolts can be set in the wet concrete.

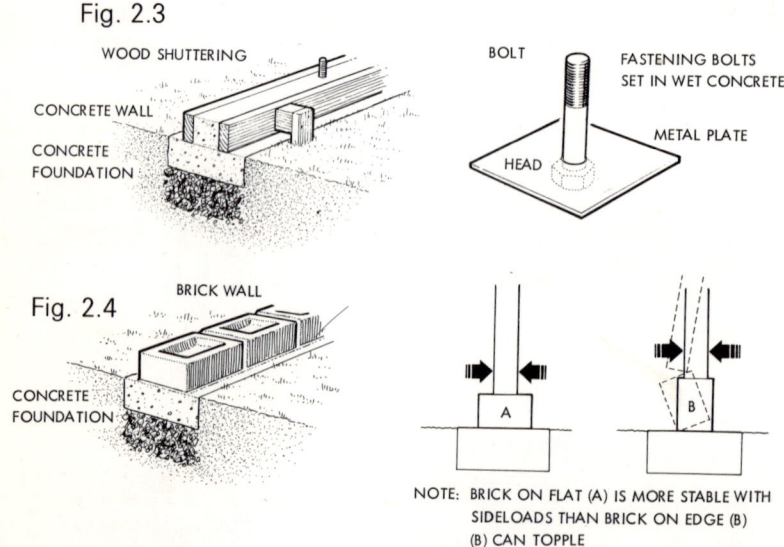

Fig. 2.3

WOOD SHUTTERING

CONCRETE WALL

CONCRETE FOUNDATION

BOLT

FASTENING BOLTS SET IN WET CONCRETE

METAL PLATE

HEAD

Fig. 2.4

BRICK WALL

CONCRETE FOUNDATION

A

B

NOTE: BRICK ON FLAT (A) IS MORE STABLE WITH SIDELOADS THAN BRICK ON EDGE (B) (B) CAN TOPPLE

In the case of a wooden greenhouse it is desirable that the lowest part of the timber framing be kept several inches above the soil as a protective measure. A height of as much as 6 in. is recommended, although it can be lower. Such a wall can be poured from concrete on top of the main foundation, or built up from bricks—Fig. 2.4.

In the latter case, two layers of brick are preferable to one brick stood on edge. The former is the more stable arrangement, capable of resisting side loads, such as could be imparted by wind force on the greenhouse side, or the normal side load inherent with a Dutch type greenhouse with sloping sides. A single brick on edge will tend to topple under such loads, placing a premium on the strength of the mortaring. Brickwork (laid flat) can, of course, be extended upwards to complete dwarf walls.

Fastening to brickwork is more difficult than to concrete (where suitable bolts or fastenings can be inset in the wet concrete), and so concrete is usually preferred for amateur work. It also requires less skill and takes less time to complete the foundations.

Various proprietary concrete sections are also produced for greenhouse 'base walls'. These are usually of wedge shape, with the base greater than the weight to provide stability. Such plinth sections are produced in standard lengths and are usually predrilled for fastening bolts, etc. They can be cemented directly to the main foundation in a similar manner to a brick wall or may be stable enough on their own resting on rubble. Some sections include water stops and drip edges designed to ensure that the bottom of timber frames will not rest in trapped water, and thus cannot become waterloged—see Fig. 2.5.

Proportions for the foundation are determined by the true overall size of the complete framework at base level. It is thus important to know these dimensions when making a foundation for a prefabricated greenhouse—Fig. 2.6. Starting from scratch the foundation proportions can be taken off the original drawing, and if any

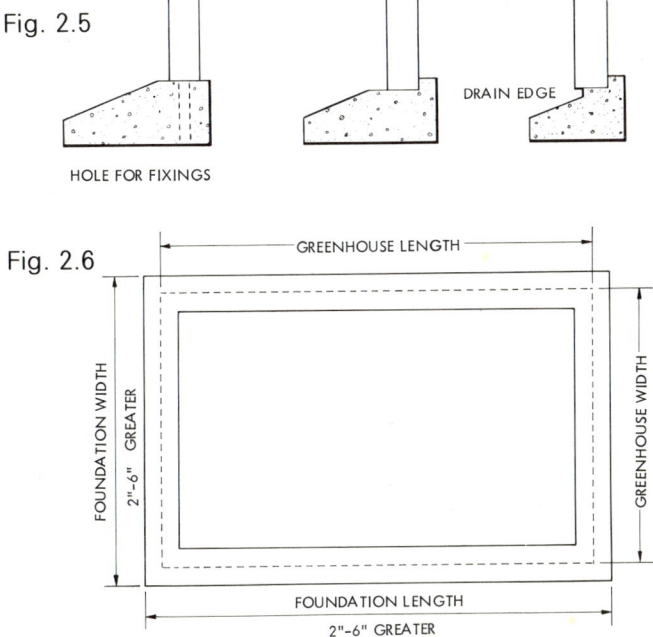

Fig. 2.5

DRAIN EDGE

HOLE FOR FIXINGS

Fig. 2.6

GREENHOUSE LENGTH

FOUNDATION WIDTH

2"–6" GREATER

GREENHOUSE WIDTH

FOUNDATION LENGTH

2"–6" GREATER

error is made this can be compensated later by 'adjusting' the size of the building as it progresses. Some amateurs in fact may not bother with a dimensioned plan at all to start with, but work from a rough sketch. The foundation is made first and the framework then literally proportioned around this.

The Greenhouse Floor

With a simple foundation for the walls the whole of the floor inside the greenhouse can be soil. This is an advantage in a glass-to-ground house since plants can be planted directly in the 'floor' on each side. However the centre needs to be a solid 'dry' area on which to stand, and this can be achieved in several ways.

Probably the simplest way is to lay a series of flagstones or paving stones down the centre of the greenhouse, on a thin layer of rubble or hardcore, if necessary to get a firm 'bed'. Raising the height of the flagstones above the soil level will be an advantage. It will help them drain better if sprayed with water, and also tend to keep them cleaner—Fig. 2.7.

Another method is to excavate the centre part of the floor to a depth of several inches and fill with gravel, clinker, stones, etc., to form a soakaway to assist drainage. The whole 'standing area' is then covered with a layer of $\frac{1}{2}$-inch chippings to a depth of 4 to 6 inches. Similar treatment can, of course, be extended to the whole floor area of a dwarf wall or half boarded greenhouse where no planting is to be done directly in the soil. This will generally keep the greenhouse cleaner and tidier than having a part soil floor.

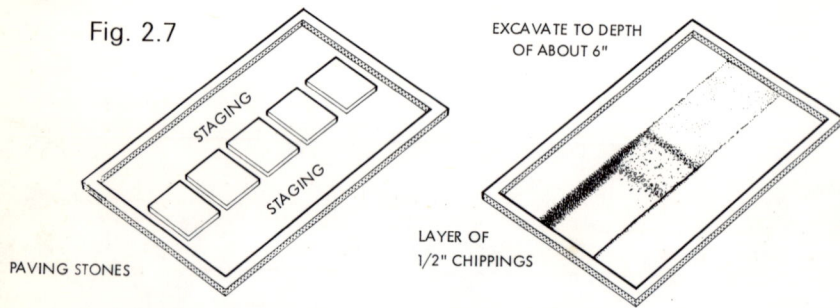

Fig. 2.7

EXCAVATE TO DEPTH OF ABOUT 6"

STAGING

STAGING

PAVING STONES

LAYER OF 1/2" CHIPPINGS

An overall concrete floor is not recommended for a greenhouse, incidentally, particularly a small greenhouse. It tends to make a greenhouse much too hot in summer, and also tends to make it dry out. The labour—and cost—of making a complete concrete plinth as a foundation for a greenhouse is thus both unnecessary and undesirable.

Tables II and III summarise some useful information on concrete and mortar mixes.

TABLE II. CONCRETE MIX FOR FOUNDATIONS

Constituent	Proportions	Working quantities per 1 cwt of cement
Cement	1 part	(1 cwt)
'Building' Sand	2 parts	3 cu ft.
Coarse Aggregate	4–5 parts	6–7 cu. ft.
Water	—	5–6 gallons

The above makes approx. 6 cu. ft. of concrete

*Sand and aggregate are normally sold by volume—i.e. cubic yards

TABLE III. MORTAR MIX FOR BRICKLAYING

Constituent	Proportions	Working quantities per 1 cwt of cement
Cement	1 part	(1 cwt)
Sharp Sand	2–3 parts	3 cu. ft.
Water	—	to make a stiff paste

The above makes approx. 4 cu. ft. of mortar

Suitable proportions and overall dimensions can be worked out as explained in Chapter 1. To render in terms of practical construction the overall shape must be divided into a number of frames. Construction can then follow conventional building

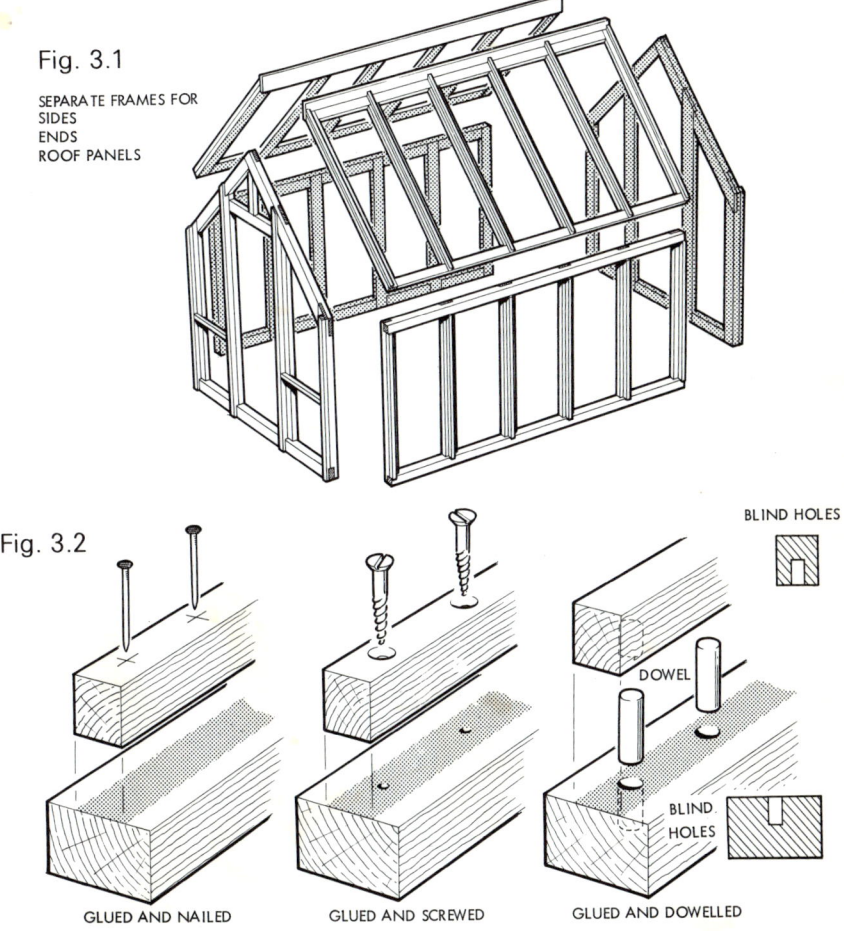

Fig. 3.1

SEPARATE FRAMES FOR
SIDES
ENDS
ROOF PANELS

Fig. 3.2

BLIND HOLES

DOWEL

BLIND HOLES

GLUED AND NAILED   GLUED AND SCREWED   GLUED AND DOWELLED

joinery techniques, or be based on 'prefabricated' building methods. The latter is particularly to be recommended for the amateur since it simplifies the amount of woodworking required, can reduce the amount of materials required, and takes less time to complete the work. Also less skilled carpentry is required.

Sides, ends and roof panels are all built as separate frames, with the advantage that these can be assembled over any suitable horizontal surface, e.g. on trestles, or even on the ground. Once all have been completed, the frames are then offered up in position and joined together—Fig. 3.1. The whole job of frame making can usually be done singlehanded up to this stage.

Woodworking joints can be as simple, or complicated, as meets the circumstances. Where the completion of a greenhouse is the primary aim, simple joints can be used

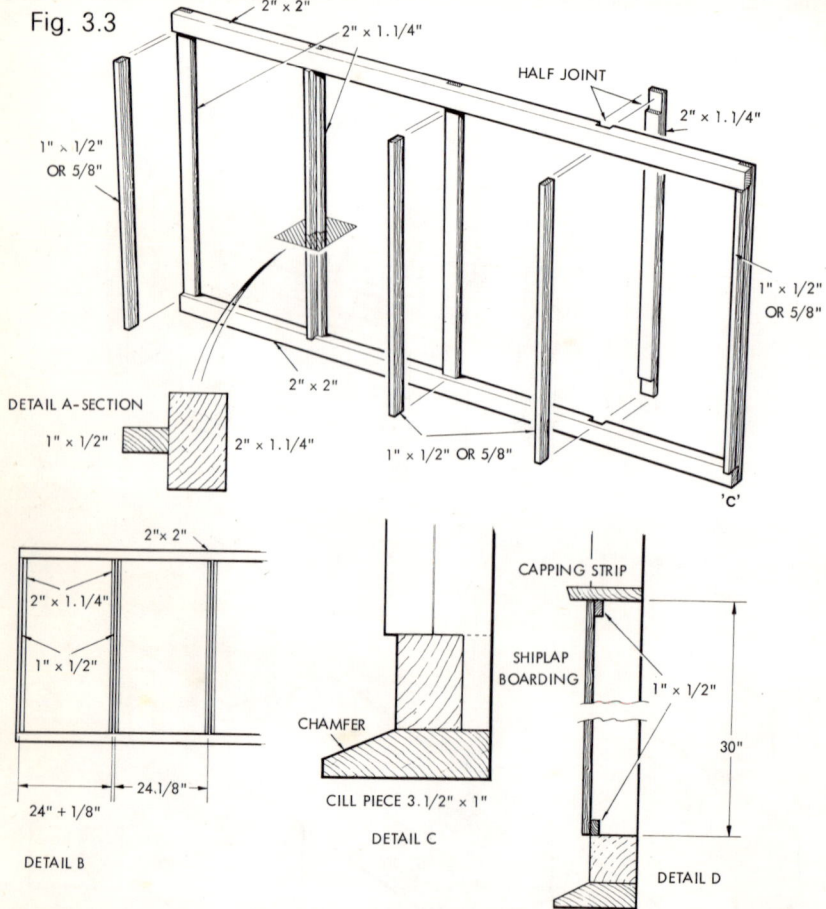

Fig. 3.3

2" x 2"

2" x 1.1/4"

HALF JOINT

2" x 1.1/4"

1" x 1/2"
OR 5/8"

1" x 1/2"
OR 5/8"

2" x 2"

DETAIL A-SECTION

1" x 1/2"   2" x 1.1/4"   1" x 1/2" OR 5/8"

'C'

2"x 2"

2" x 1.1/4"

1" x 1/2"

24.1/8"

24" + 1/8"

DETAIL B

CHAMFER

CILL PIECE 3.1/2" x 1"

DETAIL C

CAPPING STRIP

SHIPLAP
BOARDING

1" x 1/2"

30"

DETAIL D

to speed the work. If the builder is already reasonably skilled in carpentry, however, more elaborate joints can be employed to incorporate a higher degree of craftsmanship in the project. This chapter describes only simplified technique.

Glued joints are recommended throughout, using a modern UF resin glue (e.g. Cascamite). This will produce fully waterproof joints, but additional reinforcement is recommended. This can be provided by nailing, screwing, or dowelling—Fig. 3.2.

Nailing is the simplest and quickest, and generally satisfactory if galvanised nails are used. Screwing is a better method, but takes considerably longer. Also brass woodscrews should be used in preference to steel screws, which will considerably increase the cost of fastenings required. Dowelling is thus the preferred method of the three, although this takes longer still.

Main joints holding the frame members to each other can be bolted up, the frames merely butting together. Gluing is not necessary at these points. Either galvanised bolts or black coach bolts are suitable.

Fig. 3.4

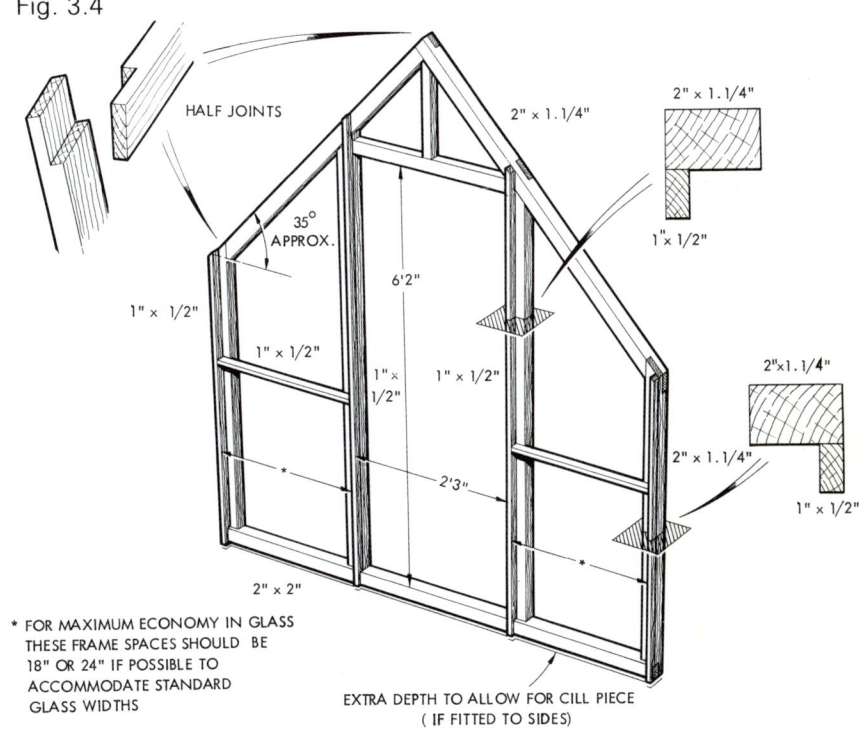

HALF JOINTS

2" x 1.1/4"

2" x 1.1/4"

35° APPROX.

1" x 1/2"

6'2"

1" x 1/2"

1" x 1/2"

2"x1.1/4"

1" x 1/2"

1" x 1/2"

2" x 1.1/4"

1" x 1/2"

2'3"

2" x 2"

* FOR MAXIMUM ECONOMY IN GLASS THESE FRAME SPACES SHOULD BE 18" OR 24" IF POSSIBLE TO ACCOMMODATE STANDARD GLASS WIDTHS

EXTRA DEPTH TO ALLOW FOR CILL PIECE (IF FITTED TO SIDES)

Side Frames

Suitable timber sides for all sizes of side frames are shown in Fig. 3.3 (see Chapter 1 for choice of timber to be used). Main members are 2 in. $\times$ 2 in., and all uprights 2 in. $\times$ $1\frac{1}{4}$ in., half jointed in position. Additional $\frac{1}{2}$ in. or $\frac{5}{8}$ in. (actual) pieces are then added to complete the glazing bars, all joints being glued and fastened.

Frame spacing should conform to 'standard' glass width, e.g. 24 in. or 18 in. The former is the preferred size for greenhouse framing. This will then give a nominal 25 in. between the centres of frames, as shown in detail B. Note this is a nominal dimension. The actual glass width available must be slightly more than 24 in. (i.e. allow about $\frac{1}{8}$ in. or $\frac{3}{16}$ in. extra for ease of fitting the glass), when working out the actual position of the uprights. Pay particular attention to getting the two end bay widths correct.

The whole can, in fact, be marked out on the two 2 in. × 2 in. members, working from a dimensioned sketch. There is no need to draw out a full size plan, or even a scale plan. The main thing is to keep the frame assembly true and square. Once finished, a bottom cill piece should be added, as shown in detail C. This is not

Fig. 3.5

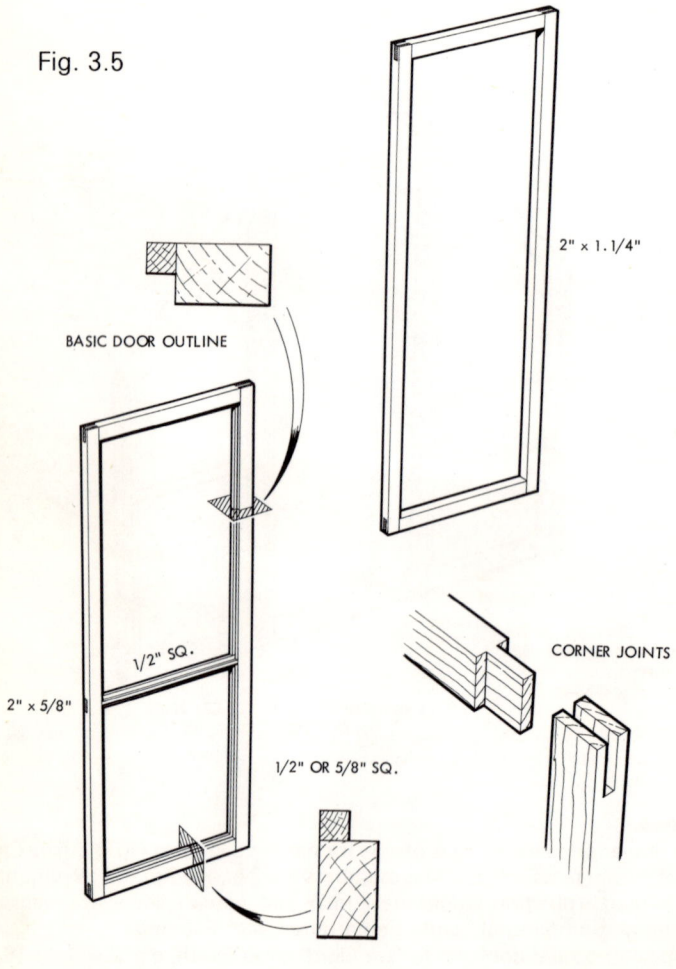

BASIC DOOR OUTLINE

2" × 1.1/4"

1/2" SQ.

2" × 5/8"

1/2" OR 5/8" SQ.

CORNER JOINTS

absolutely necessary, but is generally advisable. If the house is to be half boarded, the height of boarding is normally 30 in., calling for an additional longitudinal member to take the top of the boarding and provide a bottom frame for the glass panels. This should be topped with a capping piece to cover the end grain of the boarding, as shown in detail D. Boarding can be shiplap cedar for best appearance. If appearance is not important, the bottom sections can be panelled in exterior grade ply (or marine ply), or even asbestos composition sheeting.

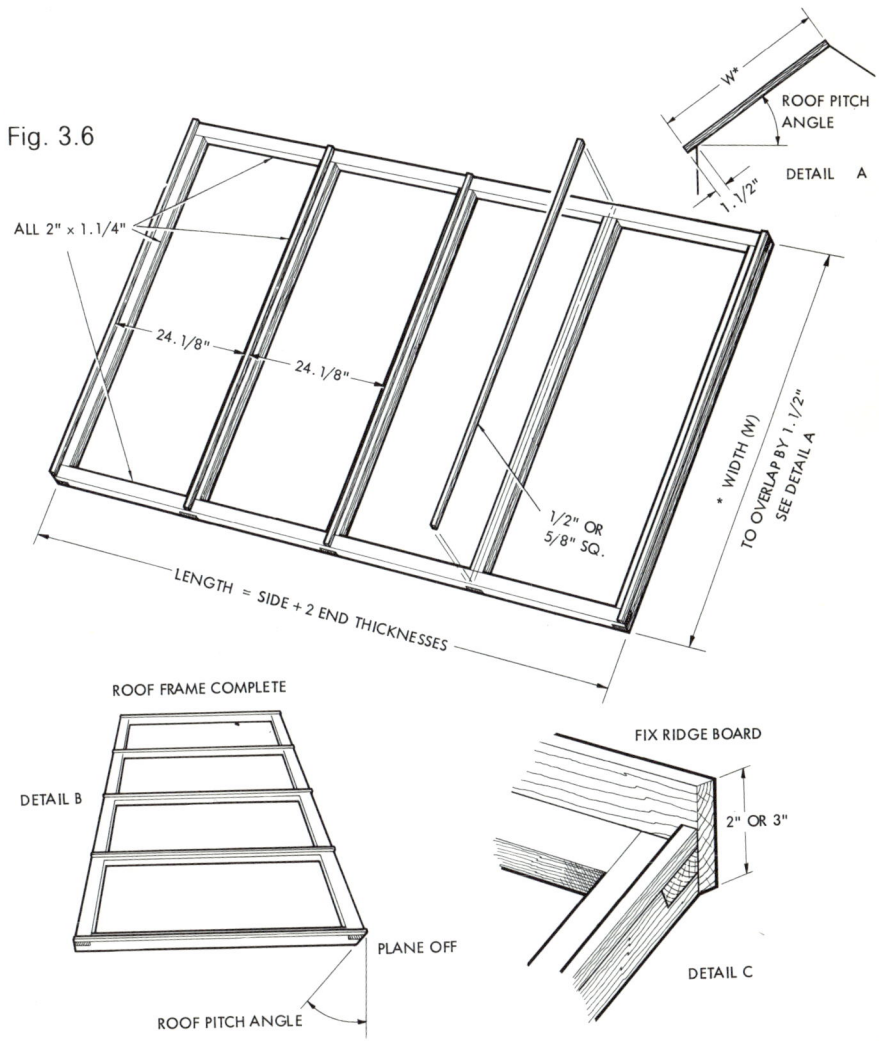

Fig. 3.6

ROOF PITCH ANGLE

DETAIL A

ALL 2" x 1.1/4"

24. 1/8"

24. 1/8"

1/2" OR 5/8" SQ.

* WIDTH (W)

TO OVERLAP BY 1. 1/2"
SEE DETAIL A

LENGTH = SIDE + 2 END THICKNESSES

ROOF FRAME COMPLETE

DETAIL B

PLANE OFF

ROOF PITCH ANGLE

FIX RIDGE BOARD

2" OR 3"

DETAIL C

Two identical frames are, of course, normally required for a conventional span roof greenhouse. It may be preferred in some cases, however, to have one side half boarded and the other glass-to-ground.

End frames

Constructional details for end frames are shown in Fig. 3.4. A door is normally required in one end only. The other end is completed with framing to carry the glass panels, as required. Glass-to-ground will probably not offer any advantage (apart from appearance in a house where both sides are glass-to-ground), and so ends can be half boarded.

All joints, again, should be glued and fastened.

Door construction can be kept straightforward, although well made joints are essential—Fig. 3.5. The door is hinged in the normal manner and may be inward or outward opening. A sliding door (sliding in guides along the outside of the frame) is better, but does require more careful fitting. Sliding doors are mostly fitted to metal greenhouses, but there is no reason why they cannot be used on wooden houses. The

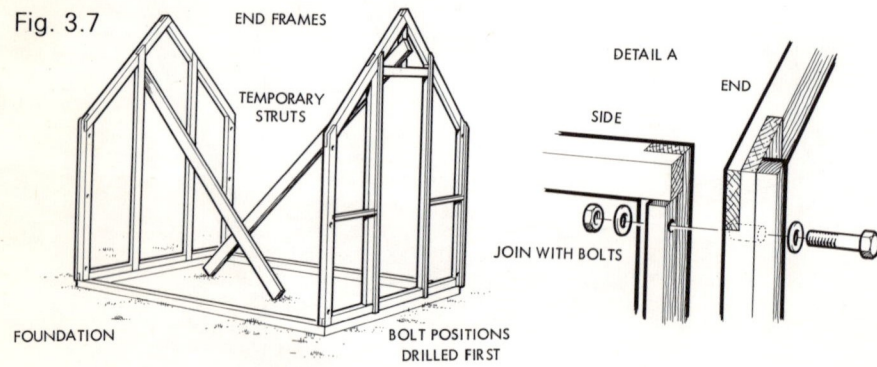

Fig. 3.7

END FRAMES

TEMPORARY STRUTS

DETAIL A

END

SIDE

JOIN WITH BOLTS

FOUNDATION

BOLT POSITIONS DRILLED FIRST

advantage of a sliding door is that it cannot blow shut (or open) and so does not require latching in an open position. Also it can easily be slid open by different amounts to provide varying degrees of ventilation.

Roof Frames

Roof frame construction is shown in Fig. 3.6, with the same spacing as for sides for accommodating standard glass width. Main frame members should be half jointed and all joints glued and fastened.

On completion the top or ridge end of each frame should be planed to a chamfer corresponding to the roof pitch angle—detail B. Each roof frame is then completed by the addition of a ridge board, 2 in. to 3 in. wide, depending on the size of the greenhouse—see detail C.

Assembly

Ends are erected first on the foundations, supported in position by temporary struts—Fig. 3.7. Use a plumb line to check that they are vertical (although if the side frames are true and square this will automatically ensure 'square' alignment of the

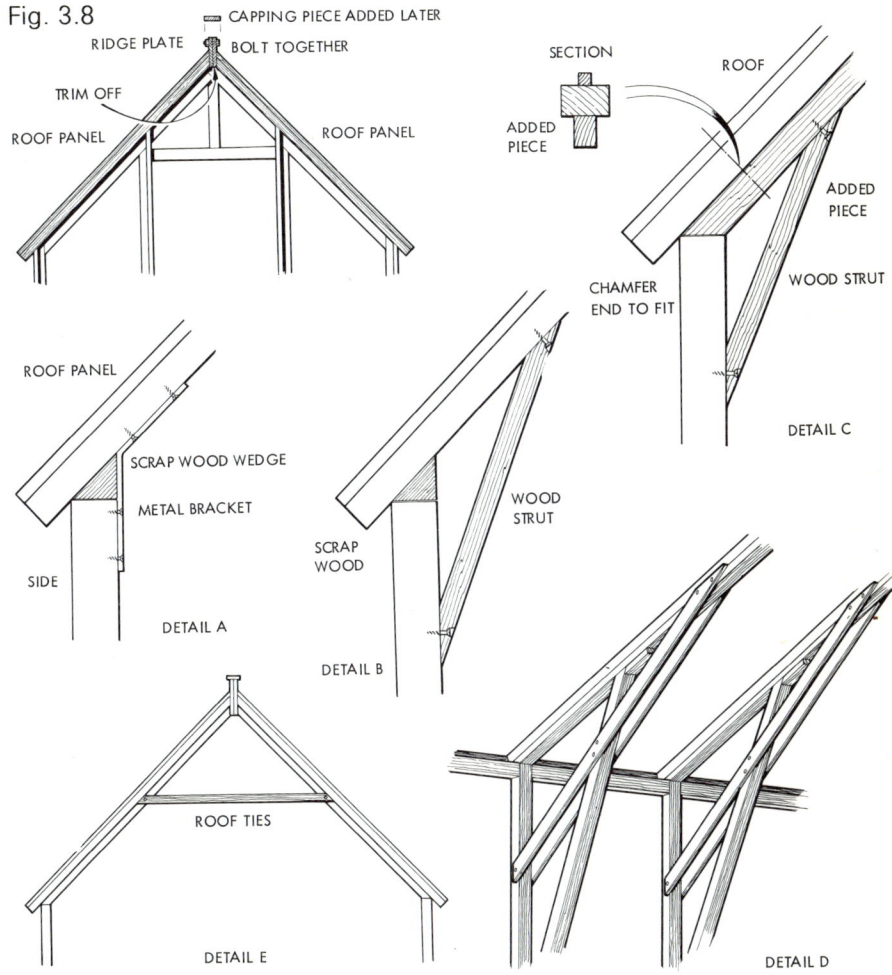

Fig. 3.8

whole house). Side frames are then offered up, adjusting the end positions slightly, if necessary. Side frames are then joined to the ends with bolts—detail A. Sides (and ends as well, if appropriate) can now be fastened to the foundations, provided the assembly checks out as square. The whole assembly will then stand on its own and the temporary strutting can be removed.

Note: with a helper, even temporary strutting is not required. The helper holds one end frame whilst a side frame is offered up and bolted in place. The other end can then be fitted in a similar manner, then the other side. The whole assembly can then be checked out for squareness on the foundations before finally fastening down.

Roof panels are now offered up in position trim off the apex of each end flat. The two roof panels can then be finally positioned and bolted together at the top through their ridge plates—Fig. 3.8. They will then be self-supporting for further work on the assembly.

Various methods are available for securing the lower ends of the roof panels to the side frames, on which they rest. A very simple method is to cut a wedge shaped piece from scrap, glue in place and then screw a galvanised metal bracket in place—detail A. This will give a strong and permanent joint, but does introduce metal fittings which can rust. Detail B shows an alternative method using a wooden ridge strut. Detail C shows a neater and more professional method of completing roof frame jointing, using an additional member glued and fastened to the underside of the room frame pieces, chamfered at the bottom end to lie on top of the side frames. This joint can be

Fig. 3.9 OPENING ROOF LIGHTS

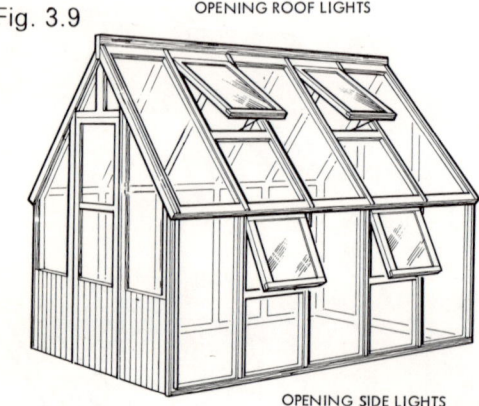

OPENING SIDE LIGHTS

glued and dowelled. An additional ridge strut in wood can be added for further strength, if required. This method is recommended for wider roofs, the additional piece added considerably stiffening the roof beam section. Detail D shows an even more elaborate method of eave strutting with double braced ties, again particularly applicable to a larger greenhouse. This will afford considerable improvement in rigidity.

Once the roof frames have been secured to the sides, the rigidity of the whole structure should be checked. It is unlikely that further bracing will be required, except in larger houses. If in any doubt, further roof ties can be added, e.g. see detail E.

Woodwork is now complete, except for the fitting of a capping strip to cover the ridge plates. All timber should be treated with preservative at this stage, or painted, as preferred, before glazing. The subject of glazing is covered in Chapter 5. See also Chapter 7 for details of opening lights or ventilators which may be required. Opening lights are made approximately half frame depth. They require the making of a simple additional frame which fits inside the main frame—see Fig. 3.9. The frame must incorporate glazing bars. It is fitted in position by hinges at the top.

Metal Greenhouse Construction 4

Although proprietary greenhouse frames are commonly made from special extruded sections in aluminium, amateur construction is readily possible using simple basic and readily available aluminium sections. Suitable overall dimensions can be worked out from the recommendations given in Chapter 1 and the same 24 in. frame

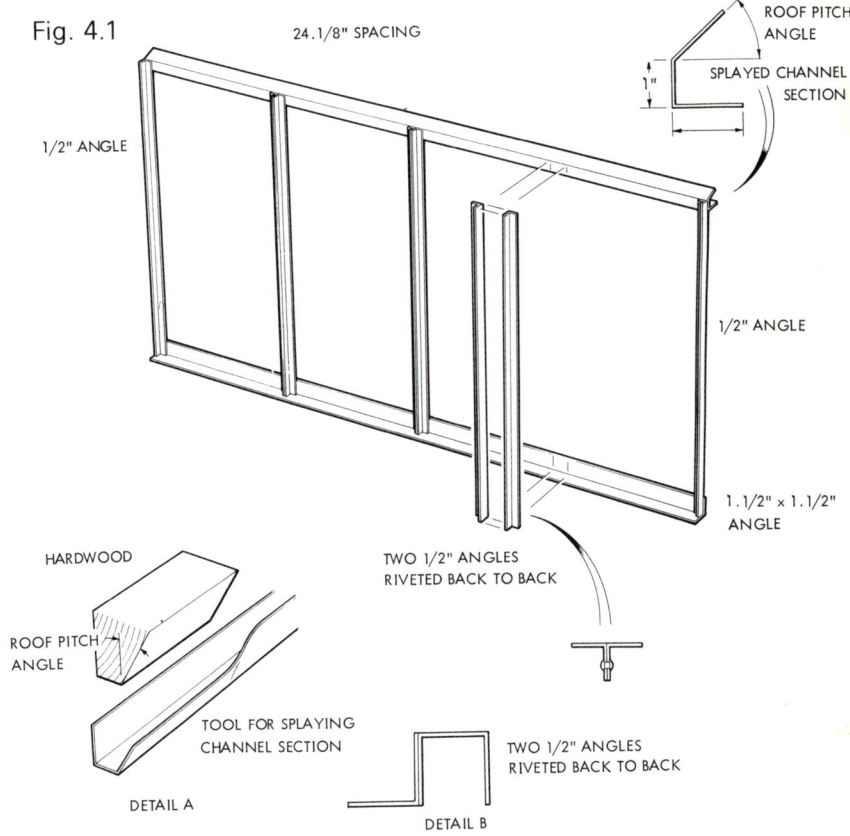

Fig. 4.1

ROOF PITCH ANGLE

24.1/8" SPACING

SPLAYED CHANNEL SECTION

1"

1/2" ANGLE

1/2" ANGLE

1.1/2" x 1.1/2" ANGLE

HARDWOOD

ROOF PITCH ANGLE

TWO 1/2" ANGLES RIVETED BACK TO BACK

TOOL FOR SPLAYING CHANNEL SECTION

DETAIL A

TWO 1/2" ANGLES RIVETED BACK TO BACK

DETAIL B

width spacing as for wooden greenhouses applies. Note, however, that with metal greenhouses the actual frame section sizes are substantially reduced.

The construction illustrated is based on the use of three sections only all 16 swg thickness. Aluminium is the preferred material, both for its resistance to corrosion and the relative ease with which it can be cut and drilled. Fastenings, however, must

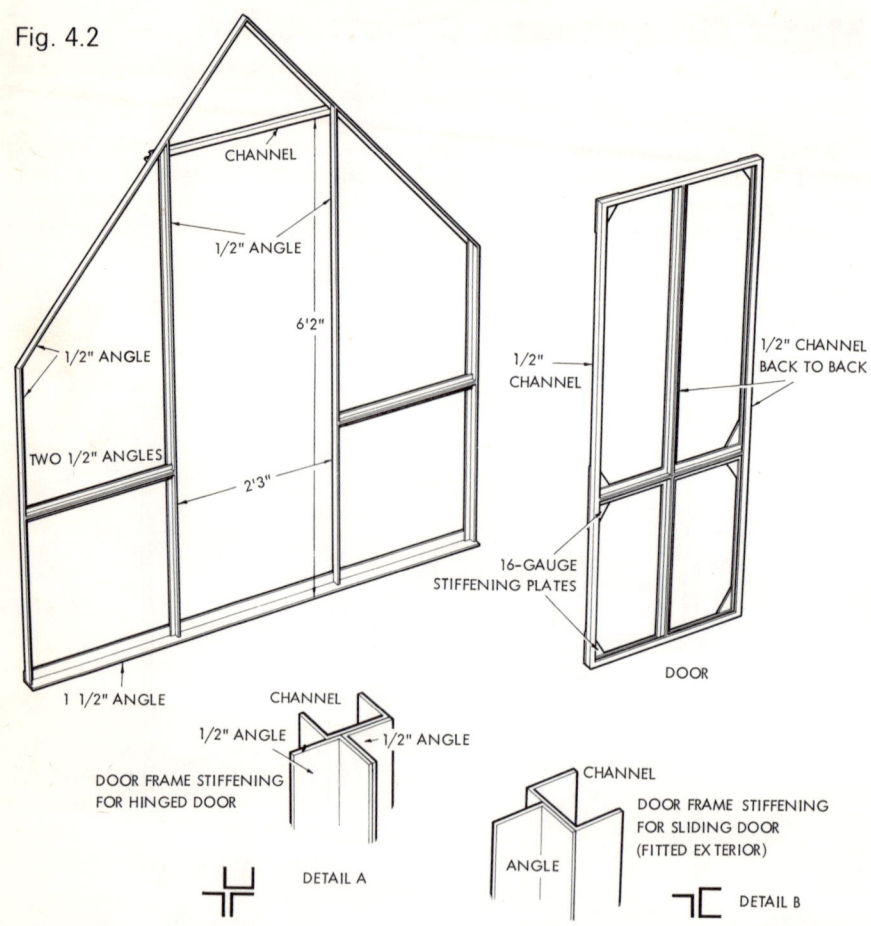

Fig. 4.2

either be aluminium (e.g. aluminium rivets) or cadmium plated steel. Galvanised steel is also acceptable. The use of fastenings in other metals (and particularly copper or copper alloy) could lead to early local corrosion developing.

Note: Pure aluminium is rather too soft for a structural material. A very hard aluminium alloy, like dural, on the other hand, is difficult to cold work without fracturing. Best choice of material for amateur work is a semi-hard alloy, capable of a certain amount of cold working. This, or even ordinary aluminium, can be used for the sections requiring a certain amount of reshaping. The ordinary L and channel sections which are not reshaped can be of high tensile alloy for maximum strength, such alloys being virtually as strong as steel.

Side frames are constructed as shown in Fig. 4.1. The $\frac{1}{2}$ in. × 1 in. channel section must first be opened up, using a hardwood dolly, as shown in detail A, hammered into the section and moved progressively along its length. The 1½ in. × 1½ in. base angle section can be reinforced by a box section behind it—detail B—but this should not be

Fig. 4.3

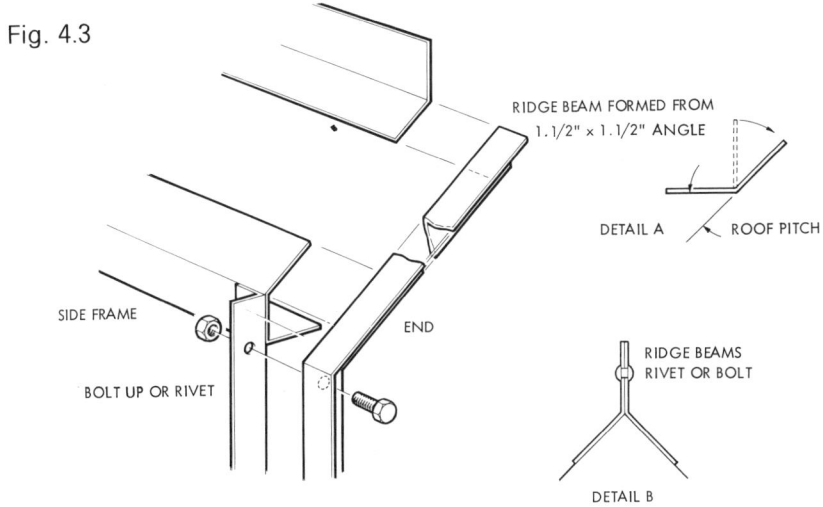

RIDGE BEAM FORMED FROM
1.1/2" × 1.1/2" ANGLE

DETAIL A   ROOF PITCH

SIDE FRAME

END

BOLT UP OR RIVET

RIDGE BEAMS
RIVET OR BOLT

DETAIL B

Fig. 4.4

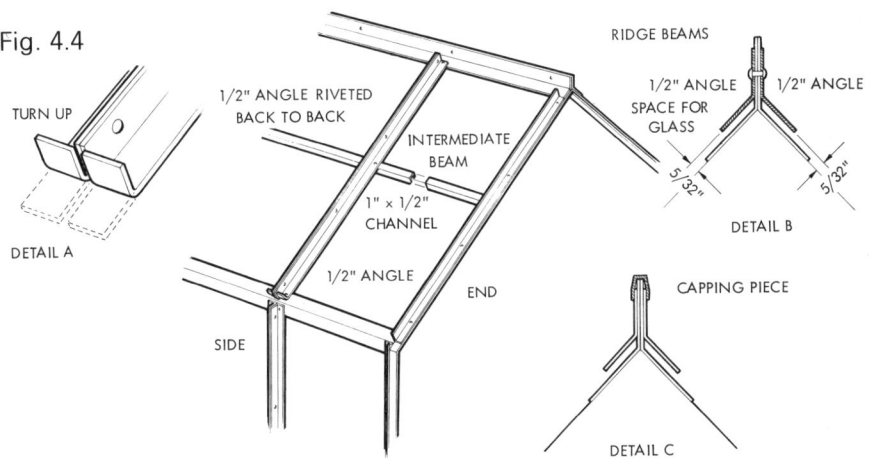

RIDGE BEAMS

1/2" ANGLE RIVETED
BACK TO BACK

1/2" ANGLE   1/2" ANGLE
SPACE FOR
GLASS

TURN UP

INTERMEDIATE
BEAM

1" × 1/2"
CHANNEL

5/32"   5/32"

DETAIL B

1/2" ANGLE

END

CAPPING PIECE

DETAIL A

SIDE

DETAIL C

necessary on greenhouse lengths less than about 12 ft. All joints should preferably be riveted, but can be bolted.

End frames are made in a similar manner, angle section being the main material used. The door opening can be reinforced by L and channel section, or a single channel section, depending on whether a hinged or sliding door is to be fitted, respectively—Fig. 4.2 detail A.

Procedure up to this stage is basically the same as for a wooden greenhouse. Sides and ends are built flat, and then erected by bolting together—Fig. 4.3. This time, however, the roof is built up on the basic structure instead of constructing separate roof panels to fit in place.

The ridge beam can be made from two lengths of $1\frac{1}{2}$ in. $\times 1\frac{1}{2}$ in. angle. These need opening up by careful hammering over a flat surface, and then riveting together as shown in detail A. This fabricated beam is then riveted in place to the end frames—detail B.

Roof frames are then completed by riveting matching lengths of angle section back-to-back, and then riveting in place to the top of the side frames and ridge

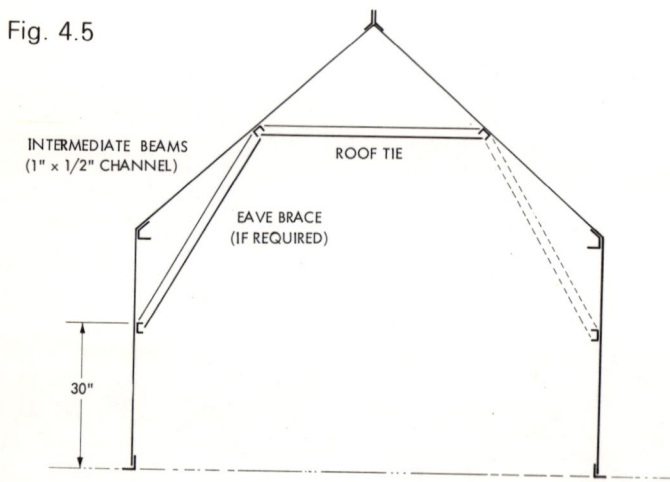

Fig. 4.5

INTERMEDIATE BEAMS
(1" × 1/2" CHANNEL)

ROOF TIE

EAVE BRACE
(IF REQUIRED)

30"

beam—Fig. 4.4. Note how the lower ends of these frame members can be cut back and bent up to form a lip to retain the glass panes in position—detail A. An intermediate channel section beam may be added along the middle of the span to provide additional rigidity, as shown.

This virtually completes the framing, although it would be advisable to fit both a capping strip to the top of the ridge, and also 'weatherboard' strips—detail B. Both of the sections required can be made by reforming the standard angle section.

Some interior bracing may be required. Roof ties can be added between the intermediate sections on the roof panels. Eave ties, if necessary, could be run from an intermediate section on the sides to the same point—Fig. 4.5. An intermediate side beam at a height of 30 in. could also act as an inner support for staging. The need for bracing, and suitable positions for such bracing, will usually become more apparent once the main structure has been completed. It should be remembered that the fitting of the glass will itself add further rigidity and on a small to medium size house no interior bracing at all may be necessary.

Fig. 4.6

EDEN METAL GREENHOUSE FRAME ASSEMBLY

If an aluminium framework is to be painted, it must first be treated type chromate primer. This is available in aerosol cans, which is t method of application (but also the most costly). A two-part primer, on, is usually far more effective. Virtually any type of 'external' pain over this type of primer, but a marine paint is probably best from the durability and resistance to peeling.

Glazing requirements are again covered in Chapter 5. See also information on the provision of opening lights and ventilators.

An example of the complex extruded sections employed in some pr greenhouses is shown in Fig. 4.6. Assembly is by specially designed the bolt heads sliding into a channel on the inside of the glazing ba must first be opened up, using a hardwood dolly, as shown in detail A, hammered into the section and moved progressively along its length. The $1\frac{1}{2}$ in. $\times$ $1\frac{1}{2}$ in. base angle section can be reinforced by a box section behind it—detail B—but this should not be

Fig. 4.3

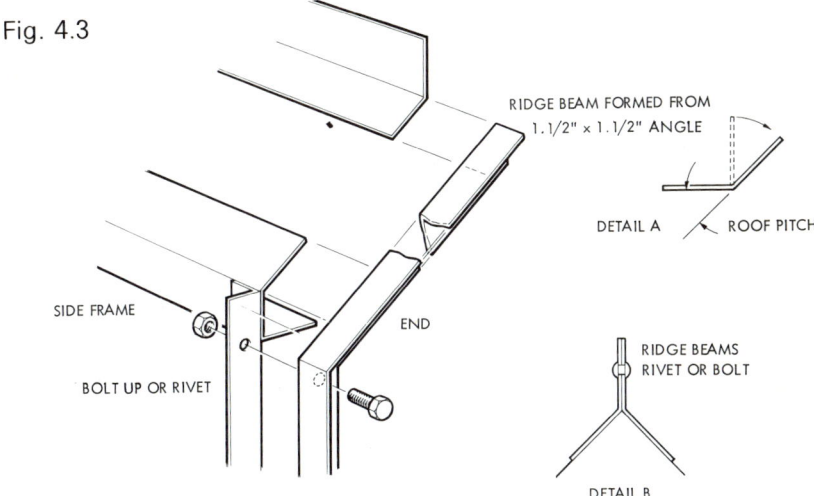

RIDGE BEAM FORMED FROM 1.1/2" x 1.1/2" ANGLE

DETAIL A — ROOF PITCH

SIDE FRAME

END

BOLT UP OR RIVET

RIDGE BEAMS RIVET OR BOLT

DETAIL B

Fig. 4.4

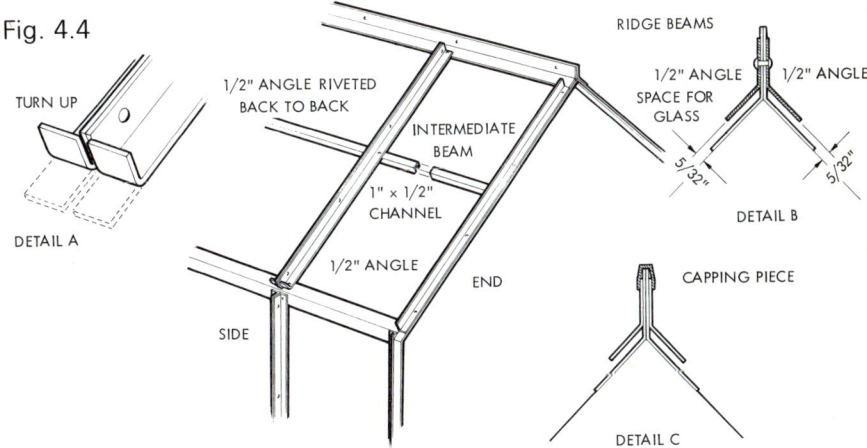

TURN UP

DETAIL A

1/2" ANGLE RIVETED BACK TO BACK

INTERMEDIATE BEAM

1" x 1/2" CHANNEL

1/2" ANGLE

SIDE

END

RIDGE BEAMS

1/2" ANGLE SPACE FOR GLASS

1/2" ANGLE

5/32"

5/32"

DETAIL B

CAPPING PIECE

DETAIL C

necessary on greenhouse lengths less than about 12 ft. All joints should preferably be riveted, but can be bolted.

End frames are made in a similar manner, angle section being the main material used. The door opening can be reinforced by L and channel section, or a single channel section, depending on whether a hinged or sliding door is to be fitted, respectively—Fig. 4.2 detail A.

Procedure up to this stage is basically the same as for a wooden greenhouse. Sides and ends are built flat, and then erected by bolting together—Fig. 4.3. This time, however, the roof is built up on the basic structure instead of constructing separate roof panels to fit in place.

The ridge beam can be made from two lengths of $1\frac{1}{2}$ in. × $1\frac{1}{2}$ in. angle. These need opening up by careful hammering over a flat surface, and then riveting together as shown in detail A. This fabricated beam is then riveted in place to the end frames—detail B.

Roof frames are then completed by riveting matching lengths of angle section back-to-back, and then riveting in place to the top of the side frames and ridge

Fig. 4.5

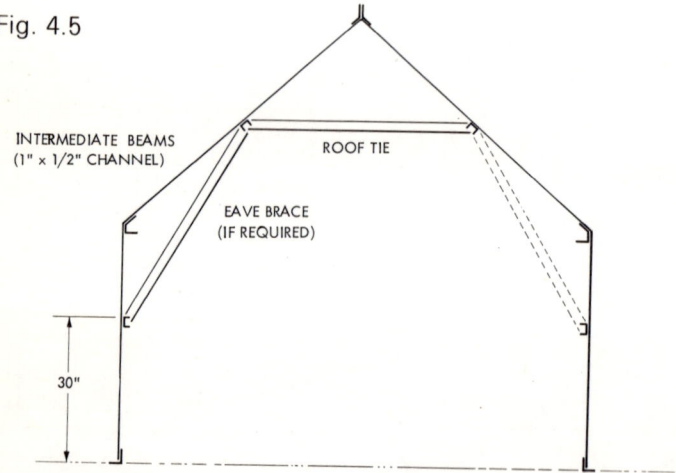

INTERMEDIATE BEAMS
(1" × 1/2" CHANNEL)

ROOF TIE

EAVE BRACE
(IF REQUIRED)

30"

beam—Fig. 4.4. Note how the lower ends of these frame members can be cut back and bent up to form a lip to retain the glass panes in position—detail A. An intermediate channel section beam may be added along the middle of the span to provide additional rigidity, as shown.

This virtually completes the framing, although it would be advisable to fit both a capping strip to the top of the ridge, and also 'weatherboard' strips—detail B. Both of the sections required can be made by reforming the standard angle section.

Some interior bracing may be required. Roof ties can be added between the intermediate sections on the roof panels. Eave ties, if necessary, could be run from an intermediate section on the sides to the same point—Fig. 4.5. An intermediate side beam at a height of 30 in. could also act as an inner support for staging. The need for bracing, and suitable positions for such bracing, will usually become more apparent once the main structure has been completed. It should be remembered that the fitting of the glass will itself add further rigidity and on a small to medium size house no interior bracing at all may be necessary.

Fig. 4.6

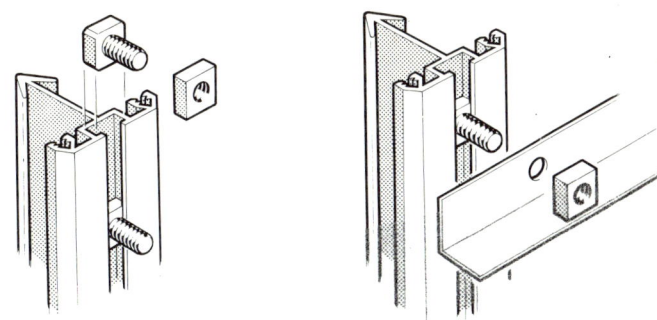

EDEN METAL GREENHOUSE FRAME ASSEMBLY

If an aluminium framework is to be painted, it must first be treated with an etching type chromate primer. This is available in aerosol cans, which is the most speedy method of application (but also the most costly). A two-part primer, which is painted on, is usually far more effective. Virtually any type of 'external' paint can be applied over this type of primer, but a marine paint is probably best from the point of view of durability and resistance to peeling.

Glazing requirements are again covered in Chapter 5. See also Chapter 7 for information on the provision of opening lights and ventilators.

An example of the complex extruded sections employed in some proprietary metal greenhouses is shown in Fig. 4.6. Assembly is by specially designed nuts and bolts, the bolt heads sliding into a channel on the inside of the glazing bars.

Glazing

The type of glass virtually standard for all sizes of amateur greenhouses is '24 ounce clear', which is nominally $\frac{1}{8}$ in. (or 3 mm) thick. This is ordinary sheet 'window' glass. There are in fact two grades—B for general purpose work and A for better quality work. Grade B is quite suitable, and less expensive.

There is also a special type of horticultural glass, generally known as 'vita' glass, which is claimed to be beneficial for greenhouse work. It is considerably more expensive and less readily available; and the results obtained are mixed. Some plants grow better under this type of glass, but the majority seem unaffected. Ordinary glass is thus generally suitable.

Transparent or translucent plastic sheeting is not to be recommended for greenhouse work, although it may give satisfactory results in a conservatory which is also used partly as a greenhouse. If an 'unbreakable' roof material is required, then

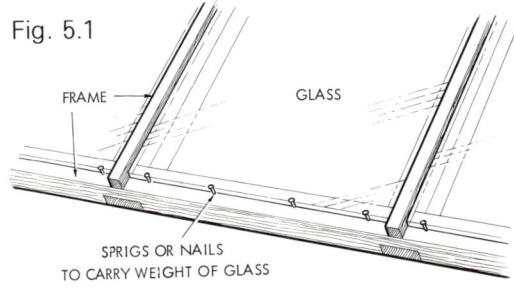

Fig. 5.1

FRAME

GLASS

SPRIGS OR NAILS
TO CARRY WEIGHT OF GLASS

rooflights moulded in glass fibre are better than other plastics, although considerably more expensive.

Normally greenhouse frames are designed to take standard widths of glass, i.e. 24 in. wide (or 18 in. on end panels), as this reduces the amount of cutting required. An exception is Dutch-light panes, which are available in a standard size of 4 ft 8 in. × 2 ft 4$\frac{3}{4}$ in. Thus Dutch greenhouse frames are normally proportioned to take these standard panels, at least for the walls. This also represents about the largest size of 24 oz. glass which can be handled readily for fitting in place without too much risk of breakage—and the cost of individual large panes of this size can be considerable (about £1·00 per pane, or more).

The glass for glazing represents a major cost in the construction of a greenhouse—and also one of the most time-consuming jobs. Much can be done to reduce the latter by designs incorporating glazing bars which enable the panels to be laid or slid in place. Cutting to length required is best left to the professional, when ordering the glass, particularly for the cutting of non-rectangular shapes—as this again will eliminate breakage at the start.

In the case of proprietary greenhouse 'kits' all necessary glass is supplied with the kit, cut to required size. Some firms even offer 'ready glazed' sections, which can be a considerable time saver. However, very much more care is needed when handling these sections during erection of the building.

Logically, with a wooden greenhouse all panes of glass should be bedded down on a thin layer of putty along the rabbets of the sashes and sash bars. This provides a good sealed joint between the glass and frame, and eliminates small 'pockets' which could harbour insects or plant disease. An external fillet of putty is also desirable, but not essential. Much time can be saved by eliminating this, especially if the constructor is not neat with putty work. Quadrant moulding can be used instead, pinned in place.

Panes should be held in place by springs or brads nailed into the frame. Brads are also needed at the bottom of the frame to hold roof panes in place—Fig. 5.1.

Rather than use large panes through corresponding to the full panel sizes, some economy is often possible using shorter length panes as these can often be purchased

Fig. 5.2

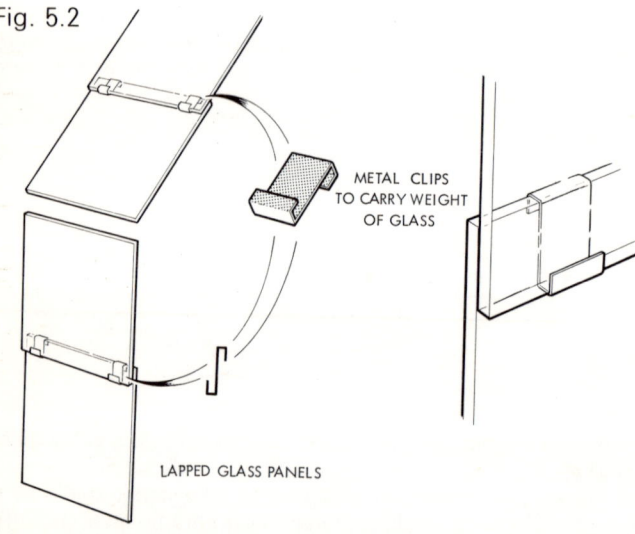

METAL CLIPS TO CARRY WEIGHT OF GLASS

LAPPED GLASS PANELS

as standard sizes, requiring no cutting. In this case glass joints should be lapped and metal clips used as shown in Fig. 5.2 to prevent sliding. These clips will transfer the weight of the panes downwards, and finally onto the cill on which the lower pane rests.

Without them, individual panes could slip down out of position, for example, in hot weather softening the putty. Note that the overlap should always be with the top pane outermost to avoid rain being driven through. The metal clips themselves can be cut from sheet aluminium, copper or zinc, all of these metals being resistant to corrosion.

Alternative to puttying, special glazing material available in the form of strips can be used. This is more expensive, but very much simpler to use on conventional wooden frames. Proprietary frames may also include special glazing bars into which the glass panes can be slipped without 'sealing', although this normally applies in the case of metal greenhouses.

A method of modifying the glazing bars used with the simple greenhouse frame construction described in Chapter 3 is shown in Fig. 5.3. This involves making the framework flush and adjusting the depth of bars used in the assembly to slightly greater than that of the glass thickness to be used—say $\frac{3}{16}$ in.—then fitting them with a capping strip to form grooves into which the glass can be slid. Greater clearance will have to be allowed for lapped joints, and panes in this case may require additional wedging once slid in place to prevent them lifting or rattling.

Fig. 5.3

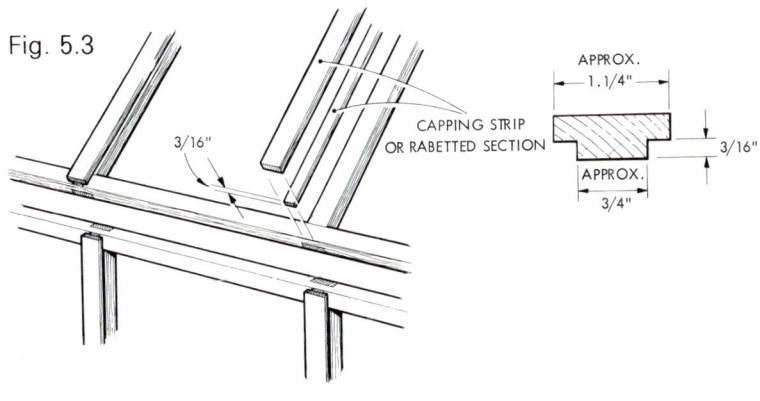

Fig. 5.4

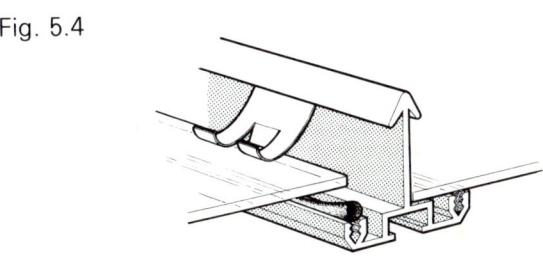

EXAMPLE OF PROPRIETARY GLAZING BARS (EDEN)

Direct glazing without puttying can also be attempted on a wooden greenhouse, to save time and labour, fixing the panes with springs and clips. This can prove quite satisfactory with cedarwood framing although some 'growth' will inevitably collect between the wood and glass edges in time. The principal attraction of this straightforward method of glazing is that it does save a considerable amount of time.

Metal framed greenhouses are designed with special sections which enable the panels to be simply laid or slid in place, finally held by clips. Sealing down with putty is quite unnecessary, and thus the whole process of glazing is considerably speeded up. An example of glazing of this type with proprietary frame sections is shown in Fig. 5.4.

Sections into which the panes are laid are generally easier to cope with than slide-in sections, particularly where large panes may be involved (increasing the risk of breakage through 'bending'), or where space for offering up in position is limited. With open frame sections, however, the glass must be held in place with capping strips, or similar clips to prevent lifting.

This applies in the case of the metal frame construction described in Chapter 4. The most positive form of fixing is a light metal capping strip, which can be wired in place through holes drilled at various points along its length (corresponding to hole positions already drilled in the glazing bars)—Fig. 5.5. There are simpler methods. For example, just holes drilled in the glazing bars can be fitted with pegs or short lengths

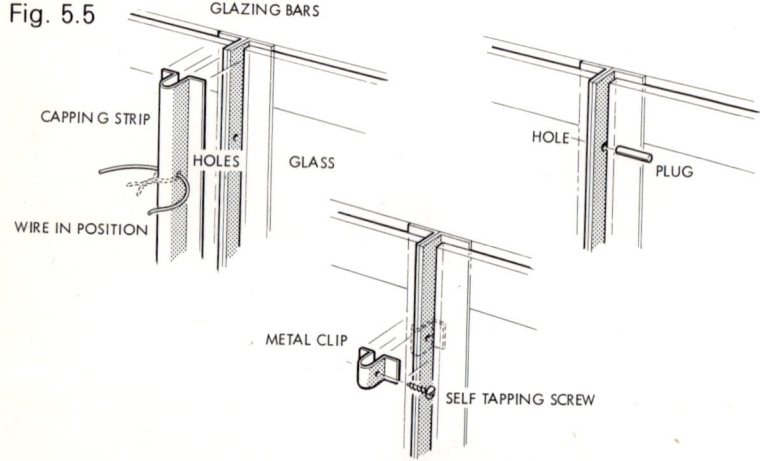

Fig. 5.5

of tight fitting metal wire to hold the glass down; or individual metal clips can be fastened to the glazing bars at suitable intervals with self tapping screws (cadmium plated in the case of aluminium frames). The latter is a very flexible arrangement where lapped glass panes are to be fitted. This, of course, also demands the use of metal clips to carry the weight of the individual panes in a vertical or down sloping direction, as in Fig. 5.2.

There appears to be no real advantage at all in puttying the glass down on metal framed greenhouses. Unputtied glazing also makes it very much easier to remove and replace a broken pane.

Fitting out the Inside 6

A form of slatted shelving, called *staging,* is needed inside any greenhouse to support pots, etc. at a suitable height. This applies even in a glass-to-ground house as not all the plants will be grown directly in the ground. Sections of staging can be removed to accommodate this, as necessary.

The recommended height for staging is usually 30 in., equivalent to normal 'workbench' height. This is a little low for taller people and to avoid a lot of bending the height of staging can be increased, although this will decrease the growing space available between the staging and roof.

Fig. 6.1

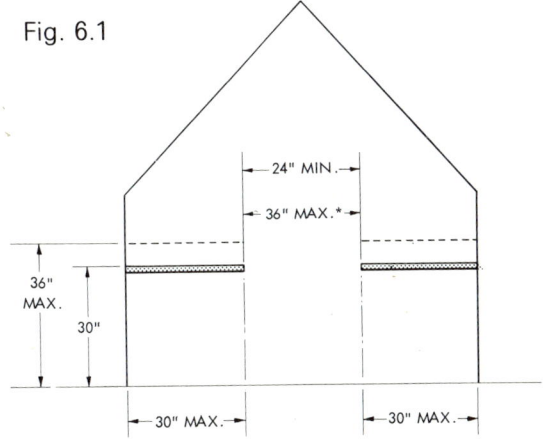

* TO UTILISE MAXIMUM GROWING AREA

The width of staging is normally governed by the width of the greenhouse. In a span house (or Dutch House) staging is normally run down both sides. A minimum central 'gangway' of 2 ft is required. Thus a maximum width for staging can be calculated as one half of greenhouse width *minus* 2 ft. For example, in the case of a 7 ft wide greenhouse, the maximum width of staging would be.

$$\tfrac{1}{2} \text{ of } (7-2) = 2\tfrac{1}{2} \text{ ft or } 30 \text{ in.}$$

A *maximum* width for staging is about 3 ft. Beyond this the staging is rather too wide to lean over to reach the far edge comfortably. If extra width is available, then to use the greenhouse area as fully as possible, staging should first be increased up to a maximum width of 3 ft; and after that the central clearance can be increased up to 3 ft—see Fig. 6.1.

Any further greenhouse width available can then be accommodated in various ways. For example, shelving can be reduced in width (minimum width 18 in.) with an additional row of staging down the centre—Fig. 6.2. This would require a minimum greenhouse width of $8\tfrac{1}{2}$ ft to provide the necessary 2 ft minimum clearance between shelving—and a little more clearance would be better.

The above general recommendations apply to a normal 'working' greenhouse, where the aim is to make available the maximum 'working' area for raising seedlings, etc., in trays and pots. For display purposes, staging is better arranged in tier form in two or three tiers, as shown in Fig. 6.3. This can be built as an integral tiered unit; or ordinary staging can be turned into display staging by making further half-width staging with supports about 12 in. high and standing on the main staging when required. The latter is the more flexible system since it enables the 'working' greenhouse to be turned into a 'display' greenhouse at the appropriate season; and back again to a 'working' greenhouse again. Tiering is limited only by the highest remaining accessible for handling and watering pots.

Similar considerations apply in the case of a lean-to greenhouse, although width is more restricted. Normally there is width available only for a single 'working' staging

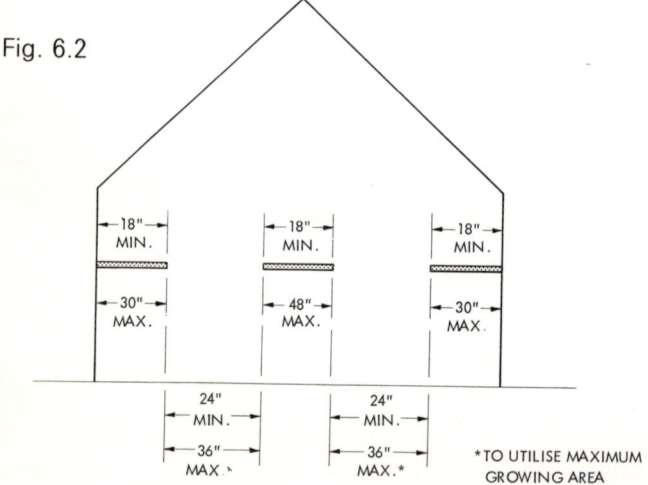

Fig. 6.2

up to 3 ft wide, with possibly narrower staging on the back wall—see Fig. 6.4. Tiered staging can also fit well in a lean-to, in which case it is almost invariably mounted against the back wall. Each level of staging will then receive more or less equal lighting.

Staging is best constructed of wood (regardless of whether the greenhouse itself is wood or metal framed). Cedar, redwood and ordinary softwoods are all suitable timbers, in that order of preference—see Chapter 1. An almost standard recommendation is that all staging timber should be treated with preservative to inhibit rot, but this should not really be necessary in the case of cedar and redwood. In the author's personal experience, even ordinary untreated softwood staging is capable of giving over ten years' service without signs of deterioration.

Suitable material sizes for staging are shown in Fig. 6.5. Reasonably close spacing of crosspieces is necessary to prevent distortion of the staging in use, each crosspiece also being a point of vertical support. It is surprising just how much weight a length of staging filled with pots, or especially sand trays, may be called upon to support continuously. For appearance sake, some people will prefer to space the crosspieces to coincide with the greenhouse frame positions, rather than at nominal spacing. This is necessary, in any case, when support is to be provided by bracing to the main framework rather than by individual legs.

Fig. 6.3

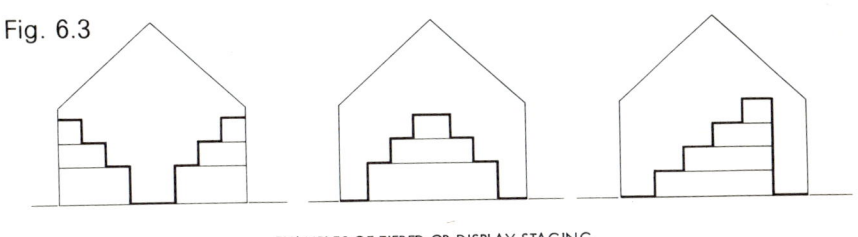

EXAMPLES OF TIERED OR DISPLAY STAGING

Fig. 6.4

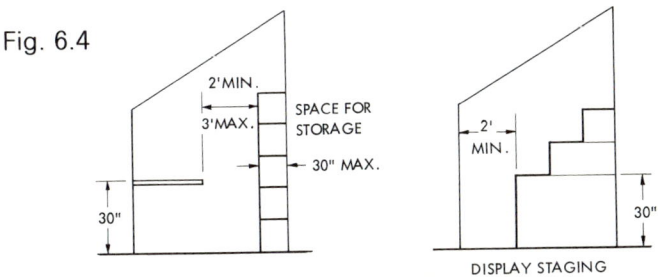

DISPLAY STAGING

Staging can be made in one continuous length to run the length of the house, or in individual sections. The latter requires rather more work and material, but provides for greater flexibility since sections can be removed, if necessary, to open up a clear space for tall plants growing upwards from ground level.

Fig. 6.5

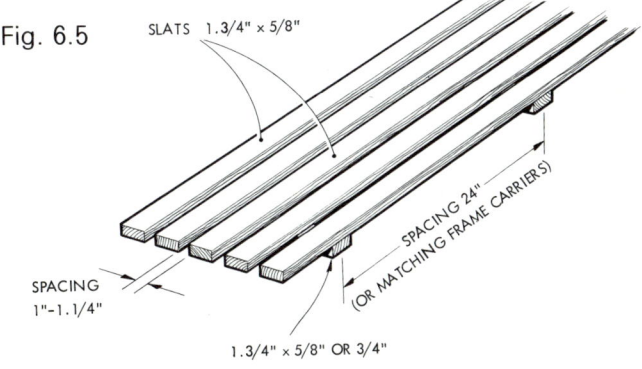

41

All staging needs strong supports. Legs of the type shown in Fig. 6.6 provide the most straightforward solution, screwed or bolted to permanent staging sections. This method, however, relies on the individual legs resting on a firm and level base.

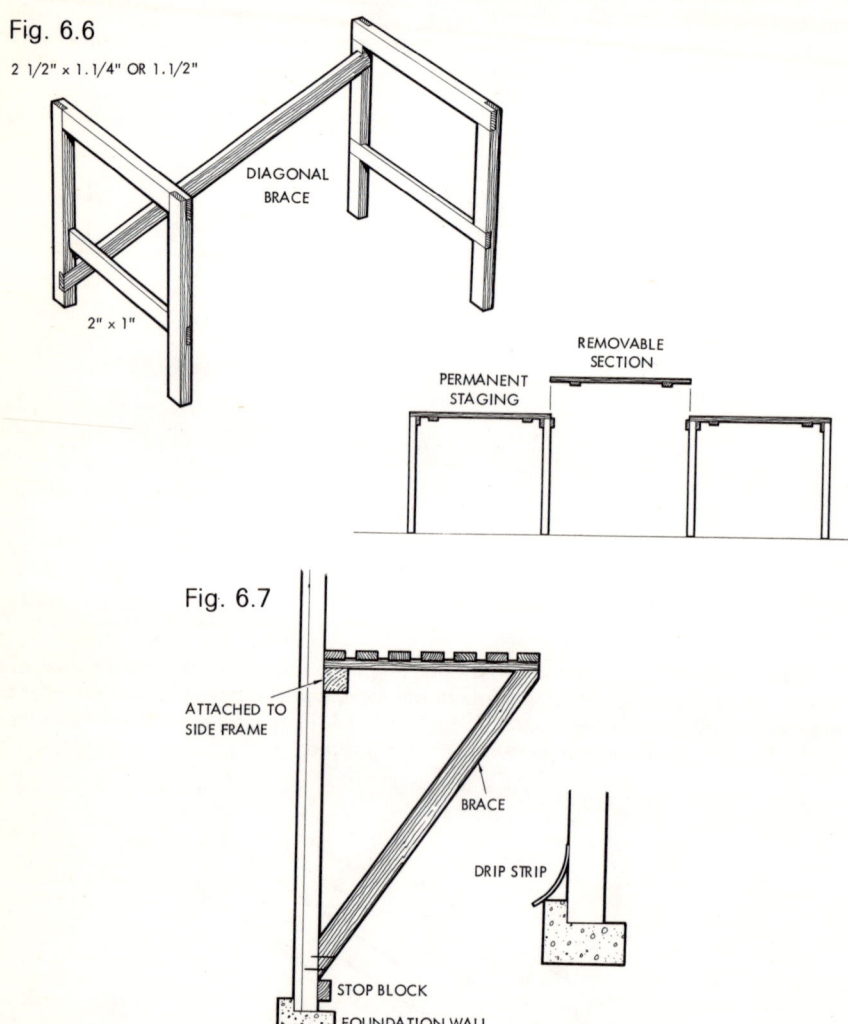

Fig. 6.6

2 1/2" x 1.1/4" OR 1.1/2"

DIAGONAL BRACE

2" x 1"

REMOVABLE SECTION

PERMANENT STAGING

Fig. 6.7

ATTACHED TO SIDE FRAME

BRACE

DRIP STRIP

STOP BLOCK

FOUNDATION WALL

Ordinary soil is not good enough. Diagonal bracing is also advisable, but this can be restricted to the back legs only so as not to interfere with leg room under the front of the staging. Even so, the individual front legs will inevitably 'get in the way' from time to time, and can be a source of annoyance.

To avoid this, brackets can be made instead of legs, bolting in place to the main greenhouse frame—see Fig. 6.7. The whole of the weight of the staging and its load is then supported by the main house framework, which must be strong enough to take it. The bottom of the main frame will also be subject to an appreciable side load, tending to push it outwards. Unless this lower member is securely fastened to the foundations a modified foundation wall section is desirable to resist this movement,

Fig. 6.8

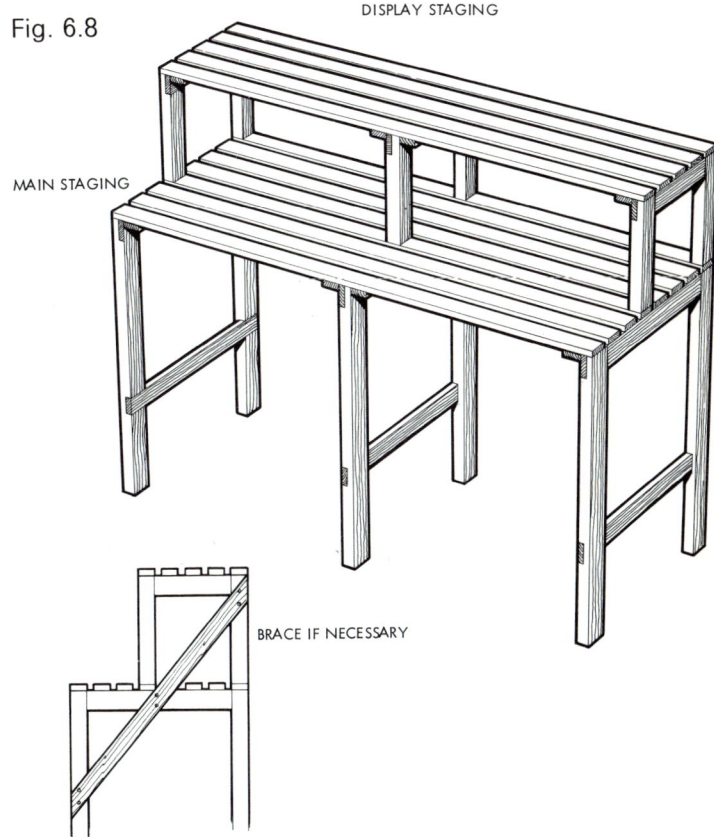

DISPLAY STAGING

MAIN STAGING

BRACE IF NECESSARY

as shown. To prevent this becoming a watertrap, a drip strip or sealing strip should be fitted. In the case of dwarf wall construction, some external bracing of the wall at the support points may be found advisable, particularly where 'full width' (3 ft wide) staging is to be carried by the brackets. These, however, are problems normally best solved on the spot. No special treatment is usually necessary where the main frames are permanently secured to the foundations, which is a general recommendation for all types of greenhouses anyway—see Chapter 2.

Narrow staging to form tiered display units can be of simpler construction. The same recommendations apply for crosspiece spacing, but simple legs can be screwed directly to these crosspieces, as shown in Fig. 6.8. Diagonal bracing should not be necessary if all joints are well made.

The actual construction work involved is simply basic carpentry. Only a minimum of preparation is required—sawing individual pieces to length from stock sizes of timber. Half joints are recommended for the legs as giving an inherently rigid assembly, but ordinary lap joints can be used for simplicity and speed, if preferred. In the latter case the rigidity of the joint will depend on the fastenings used.

Galvanised nails are generally suitable for fastening work. Staging slats need only nailing to the crosspieces, although it is an advantage also to glue all joints with a UF resin (waterproof) glue as well. This adds little time and cost to the job. Leg and support joints should be glued and nailed; or for an even stronger assembly, screwed and nailed. Steel screws will rust, but their useful life as fasteners will be almost indefinite, even in the damp conditions of a greenhouse.

Other interior fittings may be required to deal with ventilation and shading. These are covered in Chapter 7. Parts of the greenhouse may also be fitted out to individual requirements. For example, additional shelving may be erected under permanent staging to hold empty pots, seed trays, etc. Another area may be devoted to storage of tools in racks. A further shelf or area may be allocated for storing fertilisers and insecticides. It is also desirable that there should be space inside the house to store bags of compost, peat, etc. This ensures that it will be at greenhouse temperature when used for potting up.

Remember, too, that unless you have a separate potting shed or potting section built onto the end of the greenhouse, part of the staging will need to be left clear for potting up seedlings during the propagating season(s).

Ventilation and Shading

Ideally a greenhouse requires some 20 to 30 complete air changes per hour to ensure an adequate supply of fresh air to growing plants, and considerably reducing the possibility of attack by botrytis disease. To achieve this would normally require the fitting of an electrically driven ventilating fan of suitable air-moving capacity. A fan can also help maintain a constant temperature in hot weather, reduce overheating in strong sunlight, working under thermostatic control.

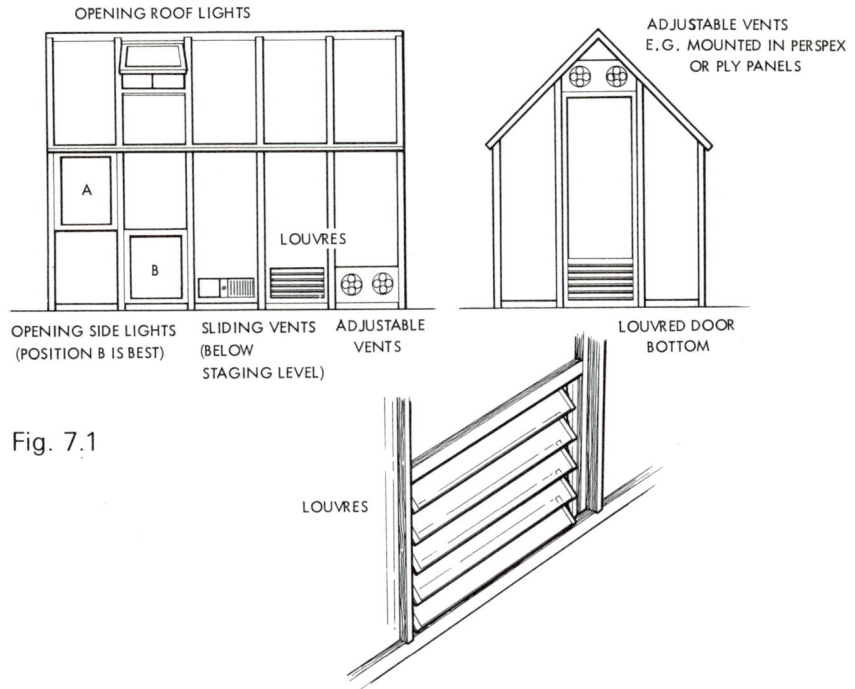

Fig. 7.1

An electric fan is, however, more of a luxury item. Ventilation is normally provided by other means in the amateur greenhouse, with overheating in summer controlled by shading.

The simplest form of ventilation is provided by upward opening roof lights. As a general rule, every two out of five bays should have an opening light approximately half the size of a roof panel. These, in conjunction with an open door, can provide a through flow of air and continual air changes. Note in this respect a sliding door is more convenient than a hinged door.

Direct ventilation of this type demands considerable attention—opening the lights at a suitable time and closing them again when the temperature falls, or unsuitable daytime conditions develop. Unsuitable conditions include high winds which could cause damaging draughts inside the house—so opening lights and doors can never be regarded as a complete method of ventilation, although they may be the only form available in the average greenhouse.

Greenhouses can benefit from side ventilation, just below the staging, as well as roof ventilation. If tubular heaters are installed (see Chapter 8) side ventilators can be directed to pass the air over the heaters, so that incoming air is warmed in winter, preventing cold draughts. Side ventilators can also be opened in conditions when open roof lights would produce cold, cutting draughts. Additional ventilators may be installed in the ends.

Fig. 7.2

WAX FILLED
THERMOSTAT UNIT

Fig. 7.1 summarises the main possibilities. Side opening lights require the same spacing as roof lights (i.e. two in every five bays). Location in the bottom half of the side panel is better than in the upper half, but this makes the opened light more vulnerable. Sliding vents are an alternative, and because of their smaller area could be fitted in alternate bays. Fixed louvre type vents are also sometimes built into sides, and particularly in doors or ends. These require some method of backing or blanking off completely, however, in inclement weather. Adjustable vents, or vents that can be opened and closed as required, are a much more flexible arrangement, providing a greater degree of variation in ventilation to meet different conditions.

No top or side ventilators should be left open on the windward side in strong winds, particularly if the air temperature is also low outside. It may, however, still be possible to open leeward side ventilators to promote circulation without cold draughts. It is desirable that at least one roof ventilator should always be open an inch or so at least, night and day, almost the whole year round—except in extremely adverse conditions—e.g. frost, thick fog or heavy driving rain striking the open vent.

Roof ventilators primarily provide an escape for overheated air and excess moisture, and an open ventilator at night will reduce condensation. Side ventilators—provided there are enough of them—are more effective in promoting air circulation and air changes. Roof ventilators can promote adequate air circulation in a smaller greenhouse in still air, however, provided there is also a suitable entry path for fresh air, e.g. an open door.

The opening of lights can be automated to some extent by the fitting of patented automatic openers working on the thermostat principle—e.g. see Fig. 7.2. A rise in temperature produces a movement of the operating element (usually rotation), which is connected to the light by mechanical linkage. Movement under a rise in temperature then opens the light. A fall in temperature causes the device to move in the opposite direction, closing the light.

Installation instructions are usually specific to the type of opening device. There may also be patterns to be fitted to a particular style of greenhouse (e.g. aluminium section frame). Main points to watch in installation are:
(i) The light itself must open freely and not bind on its hinges. Equally it should close properly and fully.

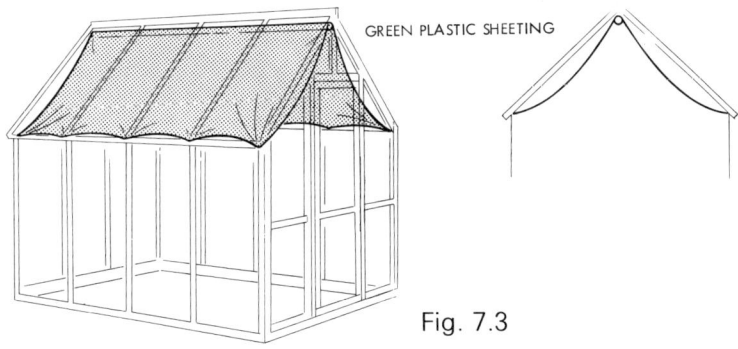

GREEN PLASTIC SHEETING

Fig. 7.3

(ii) As far as possible the leverage or effort for opening should be applied to the centre of the light, at a suitable point on the frame. Effort applied to one edge can cause distortion and binding.
(iii) The thermostat device may require shading from direct sunlight (consult the specific instructions applied).
(iv) Daily inspection is still advised to check that functioning is correct. In any case, automatic action may have to be overruled in certain conditions.

Shading may also be required from mid-May onwards—see Appendix III. The simplest method of shading is to paint the inside roof glass all over with whitewash or distemper. White is the usual colour chosen since this will also reflect heat away, although green may also be used. The coating is then washed off again in the autumn, so it is important that the coating used will wash off. A suitable 'formula' is whitening mixed with water to form a fairly thick paste, to which is added water-soluble glue or size and hot water to produce a solution of the consistency of a normal thin paint.

A much better idea is to erect physical shades inside the greenhouse, as these can readily be removed when shading is not required in the summer months (e.g. shading is not really required on dull days, and the extra unshaded light is beneficial). Again a simple solution can be provided by opaque green plastic sheet hung over a top 'rail'

Fig. 7.4

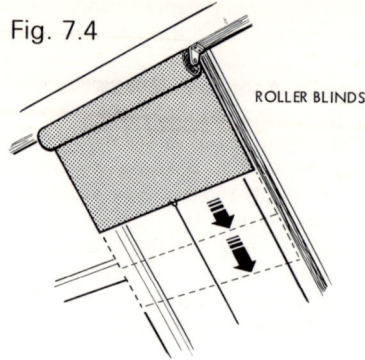

ROLLER BLINDS

with side attachments—Fig. 7.3. Roller blinds are better, however, as they are compact when rolled up and readily adjusted to any position. Blinds can be fitted to individual roof panels, or larger blinds can be fitted slightly lower down to cover whole sections of the roof when extended—Fig. 7.4. Roller blinds are normally bought as proprietary items, and fitting is fairly obvious.

Heating 8

Heating requirements for a greenhouse can be worked out quite specifically. However, the need for heating depends on the use to which the greenhouse is to be put; and there are a variety of different methods of providing heating.

As a general guide, all plants will be 'safe' down to a minimum temperature of about 40°F. To be really safe it is better to aim at a slightly higher minimum for winter—say 45°F. For seed raising or propagation in the early months of the year a very much higher temperature may be needed—e.g. 60 to 70°F, but this need not necessarily affect the overall heating requirements. *Local* heating may be added for such purposes, e.g. by the installation of an electrically heated propagating frame.

Assuming a minimum temperature of 45°F is required, actual heating requirements can be calculated as follows: (i) Calculate the total glass area of the greenhouse, including the sides, ends and roof. Framework is considered as glass area. (ii) Calculate the total area of dwarf walls or half boarded walls (where applicable); or the area of the existing wall enclosed by the greenhouse in the case of a lean-to. (iii) Take half of this latter value (ii) and add to the glass area to get a figure for the *total equivalent glass area.* (iv) Estimate the likely minimum outside temperature anticipated for your locality. If in doubt, use a figure of 20°F. It does not matter if you have 'underestimated' and you are working to a lower figure than actually reached. It is better to be on the safe side in any case. With thermostat control of heating you will not use any more heating than necessary. (v) Work out the temperature difference involved—e.g. 45 −20 = 25°F. (vi) Work out the amount of heat required from the following formula(s).

Heat required = equivalent glass area (sq. ft) × temp. diff. (25) × 0·44 watts
$$= 11 \times \text{equivalent glass area (sq. ft)} - \text{watts}$$
Heat required = equivalent glass area × temp. difference (25) × 1·5 Btu.
$$= 37·5 \times \text{equivalent glass area (sq. ft)} - \text{Btu's.}$$

Note: these formulas can be used to work out heat required for any temperature difference, not just the 25°F of the example above.

The heat requirements determined above govern the size of heater required, whether electric (so many watts) or oil or solid fuel (so many Btu's)—see also Table IV.

Heating by Electricity

Electric heaters are attractive because they are relatively simple to install, require no attention to operate once installed and are particularly suitable for automatic control (i.e. switching on and off as required via a thermostat). Also they are capable of giving the most uniform heating. They are, however, more expensive than other types to install initially, and considerably more expensive to run.

For overall heating the choice lies between tubular or fan heaters. Tubular heaters are, as the name suggests, in the form of horizontal tubes enclosing a heater element, one foot of tube providing about 60 watts of heating. The corresponding length of tube required can thus readily be worked out. For even heating the lengths should be

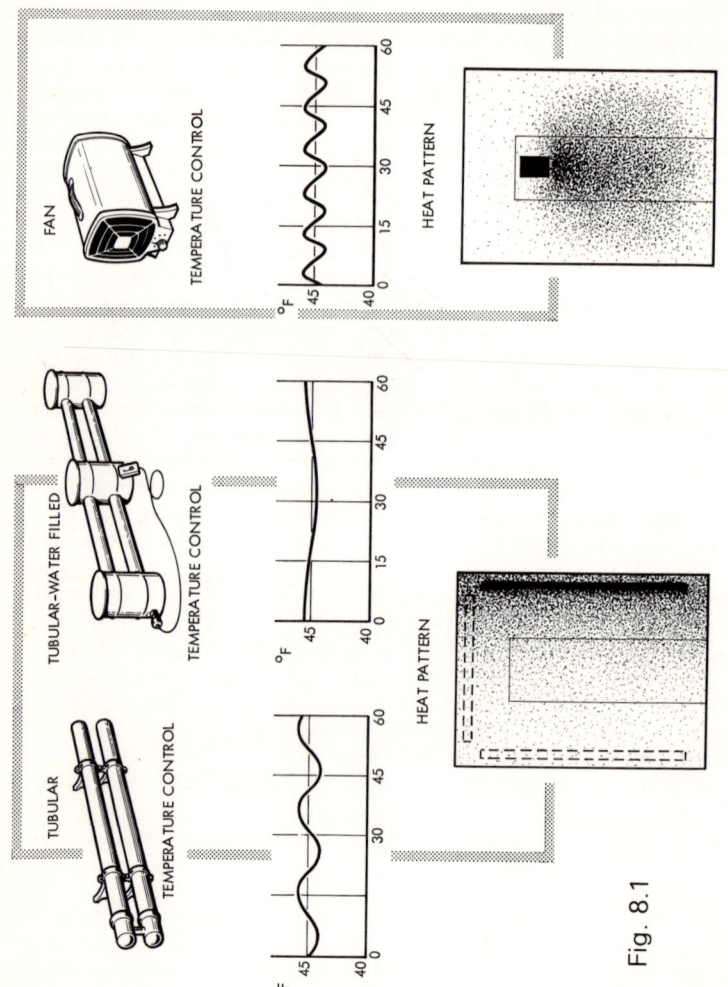

TUBULAR

TEMPERATURE CONTROL

TUBULAR-WATER FILLED

TEMPERATURE CONTROL

FAN

TEMPERATURE CONTROL

HEAT PATTERN

HEAT PATTERN

ELECTRIC GREENHOUSE HEATERS

Fig. 8.1

disposed as shown in Fig. 8.1. Control is by thermostat, switching on and off at a preset temperature (e.g. 45°F). Temperature fluctuations (and the frequency of operation of the thermostat) can be reduced with water filled tubular heaters—see Fig. 8.2—which are more expensive and a little more trouble to install. They do, however, have the advantage of providing humidity by evaporation as well as heating.

Fan heaters are a comparatively modern development, but have the advantage of circulating warm air throughout the house; although heat distribution is less uniform. Installed slightly 'off centre', their heating pattern is basically as shown in Fig. 8.1. They generally take more electricity since the fan is continuous running, only the heater element being switched off by the thermostat. Sizes range up to about 5 kilowatts for a single heater. Thus several fan heaters would be required to maintain a satisfactory minimum temperature in a larger greenhouse.

ELECTRIC SOIL WARMING HEATERS

Fig. 8.2

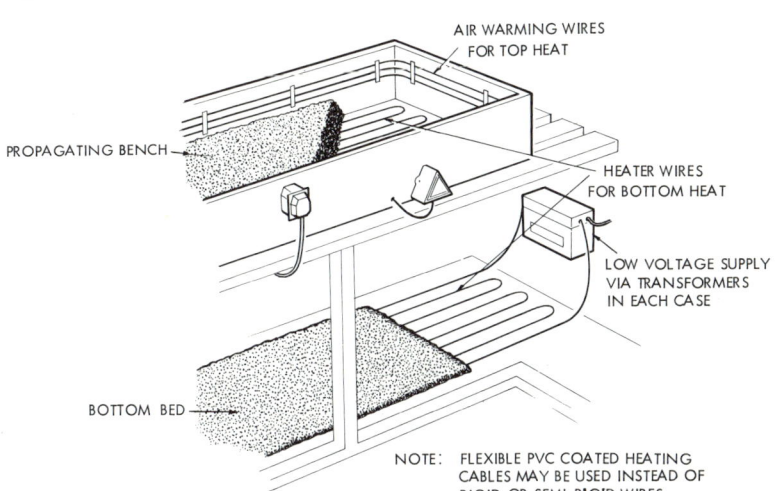

AIR WARMING WIRES FOR TOP HEAT

PROPAGATING BENCH

HEATER WIRES FOR BOTTOM HEAT

LOW VOLTAGE SUPPLY VIA TRANSFORMERS IN EACH CASE

BOTTOM BED

NOTE: FLEXIBLE PVC COATED HEATING CABLES MAY BE USED INSTEAD OF RIGID OR SEMI-RIGID WIRES.

A third type of electric heater is used specifically for localised heating. This is the soil warming element buried in a tray or soil for heating benches or beds—Fig. 8.2. It is invariably a low voltage heater, working through a transformer and thermostat, whereas the other types are usually directly connected to the mains.

Paraffin Heaters

A paraffin heater is the most economic, both from the point of view of initial cost and running costs, but requires the maximum amount of attention. Fuel must be renewed at regular intervals, and wicks need regular trimming and adjustment to prevent smoking. Also it is not suitable for automatic control, being 'on' all the time the heater is lit and fuel remains in it. However, there are later developments in the form of separate fuel tanks which can be switched via a thermostat to provide a degree of automation.

Performance can be estimated on the basis that 1 gallon of paraffin will produce 135000 Btu's of useful heat. A suitable size of heater (or required number of heaters) and corresponding consumption rate can be determined accordingly. The overall heating pattern will be rather more localised—see Fig. 8.3.

Solid Fuel Heaters

These may well be considered by the serious amateur with a relatively large greenhouse as providing an economic form of continuous heating. Such a boiler, however, will need regular attention—at least daily—for stoking, etc. The usual form comprises a solid fuel boiler which heats up water in a jacket surrounding the boiler,

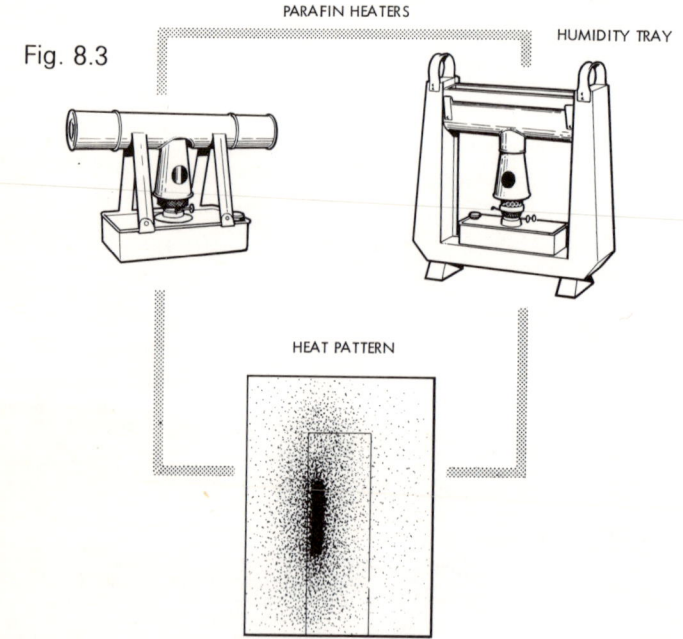

Fig. 8.3

PARAFIN HEATERS

HUMIDITY TRAY

HEAT PATTERN

the warm water then being circulated through pipes laid around the run of the greenhouse—Fig. 8.4. Good uniform heating can be provided, but not exact temperature control. The boiler should be installed outside the greenhouse to exclude fumes.

Oil-fired Boilers

Oil-fired boilers with water circulating pipes can provide a fully automated system, but the installation is too costly to consider for most amateur greenhouses—the cost of boiler alone exceeding £100. Again, too, the boiler must be installed outside the house to eliminate fumes; or if installed inside must be flued to the outside atmosphere.

A point to be considered with all heating systems is that having the greenhouse warm in the winter does not overrule requirements for airflow and ventilation—see

Chapter 7. Fan heaters are the exception here since they provide both air circulation and heat; but also have a drying effect. More attention to relative humidity may have to be paid when using heaters of this type. Some types of heaters, including paraffin heaters, are readily designed to provide moisture by evaporation as well as heat.

SOLID FUEL BOILER WITH HOT WATER PIPES

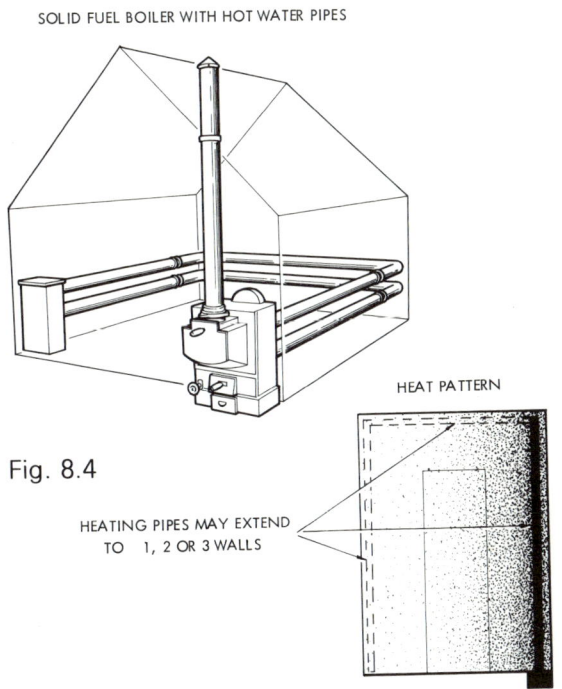

HEAT PATTERN

Fig. 8.4

HEATING PIPES MAY EXTEND
TO   1, 2 OR 3 WALLS

TABLE IV.   HEAT PRODUCED BY VARIOUS FUELS

Fuel	Btu's of heat	Conversion Efficiency*	
Anthracite Coke Wood	14500 per pound ⎫ 12000 per pound ⎬ 8000 per pound ⎭	60–75%	Solid Fuel Boilers
Paraffin Fuel Oil	158000 per gallon ⎫ 175000 per gallon ⎭	80–85%	Oil‾ Fired Boilers
Gas	100000 per therm	80–85%	—
Electricity	3412 per kilowatt hour	Up to 100% (free standing appliances)	

* Depends on type of heater and modifies the useful amount of Btu's produced.
Example: Suppose total equivalent glass area calculated is 400 sq. ft. To ensure a
minimum water temperature of 45°, allowing for a lowest outside
temperature of 20°.
 (i) Size of electric heater required (assuming 85% conversion efficiency)
        $= 400 \times (45 - 29) \times 0 \cdot 44$
        $= 11 \times 400$
        $= 4400$ or, say $4 \cdot 5$ kilowatts.
(ii) Size of paraffin heater required (assuming 85% conversion efficiency)
        $= 400 \times (45 - 75) \times 1 \cdot 5$ Btu's per hour
        $= 15000$ Btu's per hour
        $= 15000 \div (85\%$ of $158000) = 0 \cdot 11$ gallons or approx $0 \cdot 9$ pints per hour
        of paraffin consumed.

Appendix I
Manufacturers of Prefabricated Greenhouses

The following is a representative (but not complete) list of manufacturers of prefabricated greenhouses for home erection. Details of sizes and types available can be obtained by writing to these companies for brochures. Also study the advertisements in gardening journals, etc., for other addresses.

ALTON GLASSHOUSES Ltd, Alton Works, Bewdley, Worcestershire.
BANBURY BUILDINGS Ltd, Ironside Works, Banbury, Oxon.
COMPTON ASSOCIATES Ltd, Station Works, Fenny Compton, nr Leamington Spa, Warwicks.
CRITALL HOPE Ltd, Braintree, Essex.
EDENLIGHT Ltd, Station Lane, Witney, Oxon.
ROBERT H. HALL AND CO Ltd, Paddock Wood, Tonbridge, Kent.
HARRY HEBDITCH Ltd, Martock, Somerset.
HUMEX Ltd, 5 High Road, Byfleet, Weybridge, Surrey.
MEDWAY BUILDINGS Ltd.
PARK LINES AND CO Ltd, 717–719 Seven Sisters Road, London N15.
F. PRATTEN AND CO Ltd, Midsomer Norton, Bath.
REGAL PORTABLE BUILDINGS Ltd, Cromford Works, Langley Mill, Nottingham.
E. C. WALTON AND CO Ltd, Sutton-on-Trent, Newark, Notts.
WORTH BUILDINGS Ltd, Dunnington, Telford, Shropshire.

Appendix II
Brickwork Data

The following information can be useful when building dwarf walls or brickwork foundation walls.

Length of a brick—$8\frac{3}{4}$ in. plus or minus $\frac{1}{8}$ in.

Width of a brick—$4\frac{3}{16}$ in. plus or minus $\frac{1}{16}$ in.

Thickness of a brick—2 in. (type I)

$2\frac{5}{8}$ in. (type II)

or $2\frac{7}{8}$ in. (type III)

all plus or minus $\frac{1}{16}$ in.

One cubic yard of brickwork requires approximately $2\frac{1}{2}$ cu. ft of cement (or lime) and $6\frac{1}{2}$ cu. ft of sand.

Eight bricks, laid dry, measure 69 in.–71 in. end to end

33 in.–34 in. side by side

$15\frac{1}{2}$ in.–$16\frac{1}{2}$ in. on edge (type I)

$20\frac{1}{2}$ in.–$21\frac{1}{2}$ in. on edge (type II)

$22\frac{1}{2}$ in.–$23\frac{1}{2}$ in. on edge (type III)

One thousand bricks, closely stacked, occupy about 55 cu. ft.

Appendix III
Brief Monthly Guide to Greenhouse Management

January   Maintain minimum temperature of 45°F in a heated house. Temperatures up to 70°F may be necessary for starting some corms or bulbs (e.g. Amaryllis).

February   Start propagating seeds of annuals and bedding plants under heat for planting out later.
Maintain heat as necessary.
Take and start cuttings.
Dahlias, gloxinias and begonias can be started.
Use ventilation where possible to avoid excessively damp atmospheres inside the house.

March   Complete sowing of annuals and bedding plants, etc. Start sowing tomatoes and cucumber seeds.
Maintain heat, but increase ventilation whenever possible.

April   Plenty of ventilation needed.
Heating may be reduced, but watch out for frosts and sudden drops in temperature. Watering also becomes important.

May   Heating can be further reduced, or even cut off (but maintain overnight temperatures). Watering is very important for all plants, preferably watering on a rising rather than falling temperature.
Watch out for pests.

June   No heating should be required. Watering is very important (avoid both over- and under-watering). Shading may be needed from time to time, but not necessarily continuously.
Adequate ventilation very important.

July   Shading needed. No heat at all should be required. Check pests and keep atmosphere well ventilated and humid.

August   Pests may be the main problem. Treat as necessary.
Shading and good ventilation essential.

September   Heating may have to be started towards the end of the month. Shading no longer necessary.

October   Time for a general clean out and fumigation of the greenhouse. Maintain good ventilation and heat as necessary. Remove any painted on shading.

November   Good ventilation essential, but avoid cold, damp days for opening vents. Maintain constant minimum temperature with heat. Clean off all glass to give maximum light penetration.

December   The more forward bulbs can be introduced in heat. Keep glass clean for maximum light penetration. Ventilate on suitable days.

Appendix IV
The Legal Side

In most areas it is necessary to obtain consent from the local authority before a greenhouse can be erected. A plan of the site and proposed construction will have to be submitted, the latter also showing material sizes to be used, etc. Permission is generally forthcoming, but there may be a delay of up to two months, or even more, from the date of application to permission to go ahead being received.

If the land on which the greenhouse is to be erected is rented, the permission of the landlord must also be obtained. In this case, agreement should also be reached with the landlord as to the ultimate ownership of the greenhouse (e.g. whether the building can be removed if the tenancy is terminated).

Basically, a greenhouse built in sections and secured by bolts or similar fastenings rates as a tenant's fixture which can be removed by the tenant at any time during his tenancy. A greenhouse permanently fixed to foundations can not be removed, even although erected by the tenant with the landlord's permission. A similar restriction can apply if the *foundations* are permanent. Thus even if the structure is temporarily fixed to such foundations (e.g. by bolts), the fact that the foundations are permanent can render the whole building as a permanent fixture. Foundations of dry, unbonded bricks, on the other hand, would count as 'temporary'.

Where a relatively expensive greenhouse construction is contemplated on rented ground, and it is anticipated that the tenancy may be ceased at some future date, it may well be advisable to consult a solicitor on the legal standing. This could affect the choice of structure, and the type of foundations used. For example, a span house built in sections on what conforms to a 'temporary' foundation, could be a far better proposition than a lean-to, which would almost certainly qualify as a landlord's fixture.